BETWEEN KIN AND COSMOPOLIS

The Didsbury Lectures
Series Preface

The Didsbury Lectures, delivered annually at Nazarene Theological College, Manchester, are now a well-established feature on the theological calendar in Britain. The lectures are planned primarily for the academic and church community in Manchester but through their publication have reached a global readership.

The name "Didsbury Lectures" was chosen for its double significance. Didsbury is the location of Nazarene Theological College, but it was also the location of Didsbury College (sometimes known as Didsbury Wesleyan College), established in 1842 for training Wesleyan Methodist ministers.

The Didsbury Lectures were inaugurated in 1979 by Professor F. F. Bruce. He was followed annually by highly regarded scholars who established the series' standard. All have been notable for making high calibre scholarship accessible to interested and informed listeners.

The lectures give a platform for leading thinkers within the historic Christian faith to address topics of current relevance. While each lecturer is given freedom in choice of topic, the series is intended to address topics that traditionally would fall into the category of "Divinity." Beyond that, the college does not set parameters. Didsbury lecturers, in turn, have relished the privilege of engaging in the dialogue between church and academy.

Most Didsbury lecturers have been well-known scholars in the United Kingdom. From the start, the college envisaged the series as a means by which it could contribute to theological discourse between the church and the academic community more widely in Britain and abroad. The publication is an important part of fulfilling that goal. It remains the hope and prayer of the College that each volume will have a lasting and positive impact on the life of the church, and in the service of the gospel of Christ.

1979	Professor F. F. Bruce†	*Men and Movements in the Primitive Church*
1980	The Revd. Professor I. Howard Marshall	*Last Supper and Lord's Supper*
1981	The Revd. Professor James Atkinson†	*Martin Luther: Prophet to the Church Catholic*
1982	The Very Revd. Professor T. F. Torrance†	*The Mediation of Christ*
1983	The Revd. Professor C. K. Barrett†	*Church, Ministry and Sacraments in the New Testament*
1984	The Revd. Dr A. R. G. Deasley	*The Shape of Qumran Theology*
1985	Dr. Donald P. Guthrie†	*The Relevance of John's Apocalypse*
1986	Professor A. F. Walls	*The Nineteenth-Century Missionary Movement***
1987	The Revd. Dr. A. Skevington Wood†	*Reason and Revelation*

"The debate about massive and unrestricted immigration has emerged from almost nowhere to become the most toxic issue in British politics. Because reasoned argument has been banished since Enoch Powell, we have lacked a framework for considered discussion and populism has stepped in. In this well-researched and articulate hundred pages on national identity and independence (Scottish or not) Nigel Biggar gives us just such a framework, demonstrating yet again the value of public theology. He makes an outstanding contribution."
—Iain R. Torrance, Pro-chancellor, University of Aberdeen, former Moderator of the General Assembly, President Emeritus of Princeton Theological Seminary

"Many people have written recently on political theology: but the discussion tends to remain at a rather abstract level, of endorsing or decrying broad trajectories, genealogies, and movements. Biggar stands in an older Anglican tradition, running through Temple, Arnold, Coleridge, Burke, and Hooker. Immersed in this tradition, whilst drinking deeply from Barth, Niebuhr, and Augustine, Biggar remembers something that many theologians have found comfortable to forget: that the use of temporal power inevitably leads to the particular judgment in a flawed situation, and to a decision with consequences, some of which will be sad, without this rendering the decision wrong. Biggar writes with the full command of a capacious and prudential theological tradition, without ever being obscure, jargonistic, or dry. He is never afraid of strong judgments, but also never fails to give all his reasoning respectfully, and with possible caveats, always seeking to understand the good that the alternative perspective is trying to protect. The result is a forceful, well-paced text that commands attention and respect, and that will provoke controversy in the best way, by calling upon all interlocutors to join a debate, where the whole human being is invited, complete with affections, beliefs and transcendent aspirations. This is a thoughtful theological engagement with some of the deepest political dilemmas of our contemporary situation, where contingent and transient complexities are set capaciously and judiciously against the framework of eternity."
—Professor Christopher J. Insole, Durham University, Durham, UK

1988	The Revd. Professor Morna D. Hooker	*Not Ashamed of the Gospel: New Testament Interpretations of the Death of Christ*
1989	The Revd. Professor Ronald E. Clements	*Wisdom in Theology*
1990	The Revd. Professor Colin E. Gunton†	*Christ and Creation*
1991	The Revd. Professor J. D. G. Dunn	*Christian Liberty: A New Testament Perspective*
1992	The Revd. Dr P. M. Bassett	The Spanish Inquisition**
1993	Professor David J. A. Clines	*The Bible in the Modern World*
1994	The Revd. Professor James B. Torrance†	*Worship, Community, and the Triune God of Grace*
1995	The Revd. Dr. R. T. France†	*Women in the Church's Ministry*
1996	Professor Richard Bauckham	*God Crucified: Monotheism and Christology in the New Testament*
1997	Professor H. G. M. Williamson	*Variations on a Theme: King, Messiah and Servant in the Book of Isaiah*
1998	Professor David Bebbington	*Holiness in Nineteenth Century England*
1999	Professor L. W. Hurtado	*At the Origins of Christian Worship*
2000	Professor Clark Pinnock†	*The Most Moved Mover: A Theology of God's Openness*
2001	Professor Robert P. Gordon	*Holy Land, Holy City: Sacred Geography and the Interpretation of the Bible*
2002	The Revd. Dr. Herbert McGonigle	John Wesley**
2003	Professor David F. Wright†	*What Has Infant Baptism Done to Baptism? An Enquiry at the End of Christendom*
2004	The Very Revd Dr Stephen S. Smalley	*Hope for Ever: The Christian View of Life and Death*
2005	The Rt. Revd. Professor N. T. Wright	*Surprised by Hope*
2006	Professor Alan P. F. Sell	*Nonconformist Theology in the Twentieth Century*
2007	Dr. Elaine Storkey	Sin and Social Relations**
2008	Dr. Kent E. Brower	*Living as God's Holy People: Holiness and Community in Paul*
2009	Professor Alan Torrance	Religion, Naturalism, and the Triune God: Confronting Scylla and Charybdis**
2010	Professor George Brooke	The Dead Sea Scrolls and Christians Today**
2011	Professor Nigel Biggar	*Between Kin and Cosmopolis: An Ethic of the Nation*
2012	Dr. Thomas A. Noble	*Holy Trinity: Holy People: The Theology of Christian Perfecting*
2013	Professor Gordon Wenham	Rethinking Genesis 1–11**
2014	Professor Frances Young	
2015	Professor Elaine Graham	

** not yet published
† deceased

Between Kin and Cosmopolis

An Ethic of the Nation

NIGEL BIGGAR

CASCADE *Books* • Eugene, Oregon

BETWEEN KIN AND COSMOPOLIS
An Ethic of the Nation

The Didsbury Lectures Series
Copyright © 2014 Nigel Biggar. All rights reserved. Except for brief quotations in critical publications or reviews, no part of this book may be reproduced in any manner without prior written permission from the publisher. Write: Permissions, Wipf and Stock Publishers, 199 W. 8th Ave., Suite 3, Eugene, OR 97401.

Cascade Books
A Division of Wipf and Stock Publishers
199 W. 8th Ave., Suite 3
Eugene, OR 97401

www.wipfandstock.com

ISBN 13: 978-1-62032-513-1

Cataloging-in-Publication data:

Biggar, Nigel.

Between kin and cosmopolis : an ethic of the nation / Nigel Biggar.

The Didsbury Lectures Series

xvi + 110 p. ; 23 cm. Includes bibliographical references and index.

ISBN 13: 978-1-62032-513-1

1. Christianity and politics. 2. Church and state. 3. State, The. 4. Political ethics. 5. Nationalism. 5. Christian ethics. I. Series. II. Title.

BR115.P7 B54 2014

Manufactured in the U.S.A.

Table of Contents

Acknowledgements xi

Introduction xiii

1. Loyalty and Limits 1
2. Unity in Diversity? The English Case 26
3. Sovereignty and Responsibility 53
4. Nationalism and Empire 73

Conclusion 97

Bibliography 99

General Index 105

Scripture Index 109

Acknowledgements

Most of the content of this book was composed for delivery as the 2011 Didsbury Lectures at the Nazarene Theological College, Manchester. I am bound and glad, therefore, to record my thanks to colleagues at the College both for honouring me with the invitation to lecture and for providing warm hospitality during my sojourn with them.

In addition, I also owe thanks to Mr. William Sheehan, the historian of colonial counter-insurgency campaigns, and to Dr. Simon Kingston, for confirming that my construal of Irish history in chapter 4 is not implausible.

Some of the material in chapters 1, 2, and 3 has appeared elsewhere. Chapter 1 is a heavily reworked version of "The Value of Limited Loyalty," which found first published expression in *Boundaries and Justice: Diverse Ethical Perspectives* (edited by David Miller and Sohail Hashmi and published by Princeton University Press in 2001). Chapter 2 is based mainly on "Why the Establishment of the Church of England is Good for a Liberal Society," which originally appeared in *The Established Church: Past, Present and Future* (edited by Mark Chapman, Judith Maltby, and William Whyte, and published by T. & T. Clark in 2011); but it also draws from "Saving the 'Secular': the Public Vocation of Moral Theology," *Journal of Religious Ethics* 37.1 (2009). Chapter 3 echoes parts of chapter 6 of my own *In Defence of War* (Oxford University Press, 2013). I gratefully acknowledge the permission given by all three publishers to borrow material from these publications.

Introduction

Twenty-nine years ago I was told by a senior Anglican clergyman that the nation-state was *passé*. He sounded so sure of himself that I was impressed, and, being impressionable, I assumed that he must know what he was talking about. I cannot remember why he was so sure; but I do remember that his conviction was a fashionable one. Quite why it was fashionable is not clear to me now. The mid-1980s were too early for globalization's transfer of power from national governments to free global markets and transnational corporations to have become evident. Perhaps it was the recent entry of an economically ailing and politically strife-torn Britain into the arms of the European Economic Community that made the nation-state's days look so numbered. And, of course, the Cold War, which would not thaw until 1989, made international blocs look like a monolithic fact of global political life.

But twenty-nine years is a long time; and 1985 is now a whole world away. The sudden break-up of Soviet-Union unshackled long-repressed nationalisms and gave birth to a host of new nation-states in the 1990s. Up until the present financial crisis, the closer integration of the European Union together with the economic boom gave intra-national nationalisms a new lease of life, appearing to confirm the viability of small nation-states under a supra-national umbrella—after all, if Ireland and Iceland, then why not Scotland and Catalonia? And then the world-stage has seen new and powerful national players moving from the wings to the centre: China, India, and Brazil are full of a sense of growing into their own national destinies, and are in no mood either to dissolve into, or to defer to, some larger body.

In Britain the thirteen year reign of New Labour from 1997–2010 was marked by intermittent and uncertain tinkerings with national identity. First, there was the rebranding exercise known as "Cool Britannia." Then there was the 1999 Millennium Lecture in 10 Downing Street where

Introduction

the historian Linda Colley explained to Tony Blair and his colleagues the artificiality of "Britishness," first crafted in Protestant reaction to Catholic threats, and subsequently developed into proud imperial identity—artificial and now, sans Popish plot and empire, obsolete. After the *jihadist* terrorist attacks of 9/11 and 7/7, the deficiency of a laissez-faire multiculturalism became apparent to many, as did the correlative need to strengthen new immigrants' identification with their adopted country. And then there were Gordon Brown's pitifully banal attempts to talk up British identity against a resurgent Scottish National Party (S.N.P.). Now in 2014 Scotland will hold a referendum on whether or not to become independent of the United Kingdom; and the United Kingdom itself seems certain to refuse further integration into the European Union, probably moving to backtrack, if not to withdraw altogether.

Whether or not they were ever on the way out, therefore, it is clear that nations, nationalisms, and nation-states are now back, and that they look set to stay for the foreseeable future. This, therefore, seems an opportune time to stand back and reflect on them, with a view to discerning in them what is good and deserves our affirmation and support, and what is not good and deserves our contradiction and opposition.

Before we embark on our reflections, however, we need to gain some clarity on the focus of our attention, which is in fact complex. Sometimes we will consider the nation, sometimes nationalism, sometimes the nation-state, and sometimes more than one together. These are all closely related, indeed interrelated, of course, but they are each relatively distinct. First of all, take the nation. What is it, exactly? The essence of nation is almost as elusive as the essence of religion, and trying to capture and define it is almost as frustrating. I can see no hard and fast distinction between what we might call a "people" and what we might call a "nation." A definite people exists insofar as its members acknowledge that they have certain things in common and own or participate in them together. Usually these things include language, religion, and traditions of history, poetry, and music, and perhaps of literature. Invariably they include an association with a particular territory. They need not include—and probably do not—racial purity. Given this definition, then, how does a people differ from a nation? It seems to me that the word "nation" connotes a people that has a considerable measure of autonomy, and whose autonomy is viable.[1] According to

---

1. According to David Miller (*On Nationality*, esp. chapter 2, "National Identity"), a nation is an ethnic community that enjoys or aspires to a measure of autonomy in the

this definition, in the early thirteenth century the inhabitants of the island of Ireland—the "Irish"—were a people, but not a nation. They shared a defined territory, a language, a religion, and much culture besides. However, it was only when they acquired a viable instrument of island-wide self-government in 1297, through the creation of a parliament in Dublin, that they could be said to have achieved nationhood.

If being a nation is distinctively about a culturally definite people possessing a significant degree of autonomy, then nationalism is about the aspiration to acquire autonomy, increase it, or defend it. Nationalism need not be committed to secession or separation from some larger empire or nation-state. Thus, from the Union of the Scottish and English parliaments in 1707 until the 1970s, Scottish nationalism was largely about asserting and securing Scotland's equal status *within* the United Kingdom and the British empire, not about withdrawing from them.[2]

If a people acquires a viable measure of autonomy, that, by my definition, makes them a nation. But does it make them a nation-state? A state is a set of institutions of self-government, but self-government comes in different degrees. Where autonomy is limited to the operation of cultural institutions such as native language schools, we might have a nation, but not yet, I think, a nation-state. Where autonomy extends to territory-wide legal and education systems and to a church, which also operates as a conduit of public welfare provision, there we have major elements of a state, but still not a state. Such was the position of Scotland in the nineteenth and early twentieth centuries. When, however, Scotland reacquired its parliament in 1999, we can say that it became a nation-state again. But different nation-states enjoy different *de iure* degrees of sovereignty; and the new Scottish state has only limited sovereignty over fiscal policy, and none at all over foreign policy. It is a nation-state, but it is not fully sovereign.

That is as much clarity as I can offer on the basic elements of the complex subject matter of the reflections that follow. In those reflections I will express a particular point of view. I am a Christian ethicist and what I have to say will give voice to a Christian, and therefore theological, point of view. There are only ever particular viewpoints; there is no view from nowhere. But that is not to say that different outlooks share nothing in common and do not overlap at significant points. A Christian is also a human being,

---

organization of its public life through institutions of its own—whether religious, educational, legal, or political.

2. See Kidd, *Union and Unionisms: Political Thought in Scotland, 1500–2000*.

Introduction

inhabits the same world as others, and seeks to wrestle sense out of more-or-less shared experience. In what follows, therefore, I am confident that there is plenty that non-theologians, and non-Christians, will understand; and I would be very surprised indeed, if they found nothing with which to agree.

1

Loyalty and Limits

I. Against Cosmopolitanism

In Anglo-American philosophical circles—and even, it seems, in reaches of British government—the view is rising that there is no virtue in national loyalty.[1] Since all human individuals are of equal value, we have no good reason to prefer those who speak our language, share our customs, occupy our patch of the globe, or participate in our political community. Indeed, particular loyalties, whether to family or nation, are vices, moving us to discriminate unjustly against those whom Fate has cast outside the boundaries of our favoured group. Rather, enlightened by the speed and ease of global communications, we should transcend the benighted tribal attachments that have spawned so much human conflict and misery in the past, and embrace a new, cosmopolitan identity.

I suspect that a basic reason why my clergyman friend was so sure that the nation-state is in fact *passé* is that he was sure that it *should* be so.[2] Perhaps he was a nascent—and rather *avant garde*—cosmopolitan.

---

1. David Goodhart (*The British Dream*, xxv) tells the following story of an exchange over dinner at an Oxford college in the Spring of 2011: "When I said to my neighbour, one of the country's most senior civil servants, that I wanted to write a book about why liberals should be less sceptical about the nation state and more sceptical about large-scale immigration, he frowned and said, 'I disagree. When I was at the Treasury I argued for the most open door possible to immigration.... I think it's my job to maximize global welfare not national welfare.'" I have heard reports of similar sentiments currently held by civil servants in the U.K.'s Department for International Development.

2. See page xiii above.

After all, at first glance Christians have some obvious reasons for being so. Although Jesus did not cease to identify himself with the Jewish nation, he did distance himself from militant nationalist resistance to Roman imperial domination. We are told explicitly in the Gospel of John that he evaded those who would make him "king."[3] More generally, however, the pacific tenor of his teaching and conduct indicated a vision of God's reign alternative to that espoused by militant nationalism. Moreover, Jesus distanced genuine religious faith from the rites and authority of the Temple in Jerusalem, recognized that it was not the monopoly of his own people, and acknowledged its presence in Samaritans and Gentiles.[4] After Jesus' death, St. Paul further loosened the connection between faith on the one hand, and blood and land on the other. Although he too insisted on maintaining and asserting his Jewish identity, he nevertheless developed an understanding of religious faith that is not oriented toward the particular location of Jerusalem, which transcends ethnicity, and which has no proper interest in the restoration of a Jewish nation-state. Out of such an understanding emerged the trans-national religious community known as the "church."

Given these origins, it should not surprise that some interpret Christianity as implying a liberal, cosmopolitan stance over and against a partisan, nationalist one, and as preferring love for humanity in general over love for a particular nation. One expression of this can be found in Richard B. Miller's argument that Christian love for others is properly indiscriminate and unconditional: "Christianity requires an indiscriminate, unconditional love of others, irrespective of political, social, or national affiliation. . . . Christian *agape*, exemplified by Jesus' teaching and example, is altruistic and cosmopolitan."[5]

This claim has two main grounds, one biblical and the other theological. The biblical ground comprises those passages in the New Testament where "natural" loyalty to family is severely downgraded. Among them are those in the Gospels where Jesus is reported as saying that only those who hate their mothers and fathers can be his disciples,[6] that those who would follow him must "let the dead bury the dead,"[7] and that his "family" now consists of those who have joined him in his cause;[8] and also,

3. John 6:15.
4. Matt 8:5; 27:54; Mark 15:39; Luke 7:3; 23:47.
5. Richard Miller, "Christian Attitudes towards Boundaries," 17.
6. Matt 10:37; Luke 14:26.
7. Matt 8:22; Luke 9:60.
8. Matt 12:46–50; Mark 3:31–35; Luke 8:19–21.

by implication, those passages in the Epistles where St. Paul recommends virginity or celibacy as a higher good than marriage.[9]

The theological ground consists of the typically Protestant concept of God's love as showered graciously on every human creature regardless of their moral status—a concept that was most fully developed in the 1930s by the Swedish Lutheran theologian Anders Nygren. According to Nygren, God's love is utterly spontaneous and gratuitous; it is not attracted to the beloved by any of their qualities (how could it be, since those whom it loves are all sinners?) and it is in no sense beholden to them; it is simply and absolutely gracious.[10] As God loves us, so should we love our neighbors: with a pure altruism that entirely disregards their qualities. It is quite true that Nygren himself was not directly addressing the question of whether or not a certain local or national partiality in our affections and loyalties is justifiable; and that his focus was on the religious relationship between God and sinful creatures. Nevertheless, he made it quite clear that Christians are to mediate to their neighbors the same unconditional and indiscriminate love that God has shown them.[11]

What should we make of these biblical and theological grounds? Do they really imply that Christian love should be oblivious to local and national bonds? I think not. Certainly, the so-called "hard sayings" of Jesus imply that natural loyalties are subordinate to the requirements of loyalty to God; and that sometimes the latter might enjoin behaviour that contradicts normal expressions of the former. But, given that Jesus is also reported as criticizing the Pharisees for proposing a piece of casuistry that effectively permits children to neglect the proper care of their elderly parents;[12] and given that, notwithstanding his affirmation and commendation of Gentiles,[13] he apparently maintained his identity as a Jew;[14] there is good reason not to take these "hard sayings" at face-value, and to read them as hyperboles intending to relativize rather than repudiate natural loyalties. As for St. Paul, it is notable that, although he reckoned virginity and celibacy

9. 1 Cor 7.

10. Nygren, *Agape and Eros*, 75–81. Nygren uses the New Testament word *agape* to designate this radically altruistic kind of love, which he believes to be peculiarly Christian, and to differentiate it from the Greek concept of love as essentially self-serving *eros*. *Agape and Eros* was originally published in Swedish in 1930 (Part I) and 1938 (Part II).

11. Ibid., 733–37.

12. Mark 7:9–13.

13. Matt 8:5–13; 15:21–28.

14. Matt 15:24, 26; John 4:22.

superior, he persisted in regarding marriage as a good. In other words, in spite of his urgent sense of the imminent ending or transformation of the world by God, and of how this revolution of the current order of things would severely strain marital and family ties, St. Paul never went as far as to say that investment in society through marriage and children should cease. What he thereby implies is that, although the arrival of the world-to-come will involve the transformation of this world and its natural social bonds, it will not involve their simple abolition.

Upon closer inspection, then, the New Testament grounds for supposing Christian love to be properly unconditional and indiscriminate are not at all firm. That is even more so in the case of the theological ground. Certainly, if we take Jesus to be God incarnate, we can infer that the love of God for wayward human beings is gracious, or, to be more precise and specific, forgiving. As I have argued elsewhere, the word "forgiveness" commonly means two different things. It points to two distinct moments in the process of reconciliation: first, one of "compassion," and then one of "absolution."[15] Compassion is unilateral and unconditional and meets the wrongdoer before he has repented; absolution is reciprocal and conditional and meets him only afterwards. God's love is compassionate in that it sympathizes with wrongdoers in their weakness and confusion and ignorance; and it is absolving in that it is willing to set past injury aside and enter once again into a relationship of trust. But note how limited is the scope of this love: it operates only between an injured party and the one who has done the injury. It is a mode of love, but not the whole of it. Accordingly, it is unconditional and indiscriminate only in part. As compassion, its being proffered is not conditional upon the demonstration of repentance, and it is therefore made available indiscriminately to all sinners. As absolution, however, it is only offered in response to an expression of genuine repentance, and therefore only discriminately to penitent sinners.

Since this analysis, with its denial that *all* of forgiveness is unconditional, might sound counter-intuitive to Christians, especially Protestants, let me offer a brief defence. I have two points to make, one biblical and one empirical. First, in Jesus' paradigm of forgiveness, his parable of the Prodigal Son (Luke 15:11–32), the heartfelt repentance of the son is already fully established *before* we learn of his father's eager forgiveness: "When he came

---

15. I have explained my analysis of forgiveness into the two moments of compassion and absolution in several places. One of the most recent of these is "Melting the Icepacks of Enmity," 200–204.

to his senses, he said, '... I will set out and go back to my father and say to him, "Father, I have sinned against heaven and against you. I am no longer worthy to be called your son..."'" (vv. 17–19a). This he proceeds to do. While it is true that the father is filled with compassion and rushes to embrace him before he has so much as opened his mouth, the very next moment in the story has the son give explicit voice to his penitent intentions: "The son said to him, 'Father, I have sinned...'" (v. 21). What this implies, I suggest, is that the parable does *not* tell a story of simply unconditional forgiveness. Yes, the father's *compassion* is unconditional. Nevertheless, the son's repentance is a prominent part of the story, and not at all incidental, and that gives us reason to suppose that what follows depends on it.

My second line of defence is empirical and briefer, and invites the reader to reflect on her own experience. Such reflection will confirm, I suggest, that it is unloving and foolish to absolve someone who has shown insufficient awareness of what they have done wrong, both because it forecloses their moral education and growth and because it makes it likely that they will proceed to cause further injury.

Such is my defence of the assertion that God's love, as shown in Jesus and his teaching, is not simply indiscriminate. Let me return now to the larger point: that the kind of love that Jesus mainly models bears on how we should treat those who have wronged us. What it does not bear upon is how we should distribute our limited emotional, physical, temporal, and material resources in caring for the millions of fellow humans who can now claim to be—more or less closely—our neighbors. The argument from God's agape to Christian cosmopolitanism does not work.

So how *should* we relate to near and distant neighbors? My view is that Christians should begin their answer to this question with the concept of human being as creaturely. On the one hand, this implies basic human equality. If all human beings are creatures of the one God then they all share a common origin and destiny, and a common subordination. If human creaturehood is then specified in terms of being made "in God's image," then all human beings are thereby dignified with responsibility to manage the rest of the created world;[16] and each is the subject of a vocation to play

---

16. The seminal notion that humankind is made "in God's image" derives from one verse in the book of Genesis: "Then God said, 'Let us make man in our image, after our likeness; and let them have dominion ... over all the earth'" (1:26). In the history of Christian tradition this phrase has been interpreted in many different ways. However, the interpretation that is closest to the text understands it in terms of the practice of kings in the ancient world of setting up statues of themselves in outlying provinces or having

a unique part in God's work of bringing the created world to fulfilment. If we add to the doctrine of creation that of universal sinfulness, then humans are also equal in the fact (if not the degree) of their sinful condition and so in their need of God's gift of forgiveness, and consequently none has the right to stand to another simply as righteous to the unrighteous.

Given these various kinds of basic equality, each human being owes any other a certain respect or esteem, such that, for example, he will not to take the other's life intentionally or wantonly, whatever his national affiliation may be. Persons from Britain or America cannot regard the life of a person from India or China as any less valuable than that of a compatriot, for they too are loved by, and answerable to, God, and they too might mediate God's prophetic word. But human beings might owe others more than mere respect and a commitment to refrain from intentional or wanton harm. They might also owe them aid. In addition to non-maleficence, that is, they might also owe beneficence. However, whereas we are always able to refrain from harming other people intentionally or wantonly, we are not always able to benefit them. We may be responsible, but ours is a responsibility of creatures, not of gods; and our creaturely resources of energy, time, and material goods are finite. Therefore we are able only to benefit some, not all; and there might be some to whom we are more strongly obliged by ties of gratitude, or whom we are better placed to serve on account of shared language and culture or common citizenship. In short, notwithstanding the fact that all human beings are equal in certain basic respects, no matter what their native land, we might still be obliged—depending on the circumstances—to benefit near neighbors before or instead of distant ones.

However, whether near or far, human neighbors are not the only proper objects of our respect and care. So are customs and institutions. Humans come into being and grow up in a particular time, and if not in one particular place and community, then in a finite number of them. A human individual is normally inducted into particular forms of social life by her family and by other institutions—schools, churches, clubs, workplaces, political parties, public assemblies. These institutions and their customs mediate and embody certain apprehensions of the forms of human flourishing—that is, basic human goods—that are given in and with the created

---

their image imprinted on coinage, in order to represent the presence of royal authority throughout their empire. To be made in God's image, then, is to be made a representative or vice-regent of God, charged with exercising dominion in God's name over the rest of creation. For a history of the exegesis of Gen 1:26–27, see Westermann, *Genesis 1–11*, 147–55.

nature of human being. It is natural, therefore, that an individual should feel special affection for, loyalty toward, and gratitude to those communities, customs, and institutions that have benefited her by inducting her into human goods; and, since beneficiaries ought to be grateful to benefactors, it is right that she should. We have yet to specify the forms that such affection should and should not take; but that they should take some form is clear.

II. Why Loyalty to the *Nation*?

It is proper for an individual to have affection for, feel loyalty to, and show gratitude toward those communities that have enabled her to flourish. But why must this stretch as far as a *national* community or *national* institutions? Why is it not sufficient to identify with local and regional and even supranational ones? Why is loyalty to family or church—to kin or cosmopolis—not enough? There is no reason in principle why it should not be enough. The nation is not a cultural unit or form of social or political organization that is inscribed in nature's D.N.A., and no particular nation is guaranteed eternal life. Historically it is surely true, as Benedict Anderson and Linda Colley have argued, that particular nations are human constructs, not natural facts.[17] As they have evolved, so they will change and perhaps pass away. The United Kingdom did not exist before 1707. The United States could have ceased to exist in the early 1860s. Czechoslovakia did cease to exist in 1993.

If historians have reasons to be sceptical of the claims of nations, so do theologians. According to many authoritative students of the phenomenon, the nation as we now know it is a specifically modern entity, appearing first in late eighteenth-century Europe and progressively capitalizing on the cultural decline of the Christian religion. As Europeans lost their faith in God, so the story goes, they transferred their faith to the nation; and as they ceased to hope for life in the world-to-come, they began to invest themselves in the nation's immortality.[18] This certainly seems true of Romantic nationalism, judging by the following statement by Johann Gottlieb Fichte:

> The noble-minded man's belief in the eternal continuance of his influence even on this earth is thus founded on the hope of the eternal continuance of the people from which he has developed,

---

17. Benedict Anderson, *Imagined Communities,* and Colley, *Britons: Forging the Nation, 1707–1837.*

18. See, for example, Benedict Anderson, *Imagined Communities,* 11–12.

and on the characteristic of that people.... This characteristic is
the eternal thing to which he entrusts the eternity of himself and
of his continuing influence, the eternal order of things in which
he places his portion of eternity.... In order to save his nation he
must be ready even to die that it may live, and that he may live in
it the only life for which he has ever wished.[19]

Given the patently idolatrous character of Romantic nationalism, Karl Barth, writing in the shadow of its infamous Nazi expression, refused to accord the nation any special status at all in the eyes of the one true God. As he presents it in Volume III/4 of his *Church Dogmatics*, first published in 1951, national communities—or "peoples"—dissolve into near and far neighbors.[20]

Barth is surely right to puncture the pretension of nations to the status of something absolute or essential. Nations are fundamentally constituted by national consciousness, by a sense of national identity, by the feeling of individuals that they belong to *this* people. And such a sense of community is usually born in reaction against another people, which is culturally different and whose difference grates or threatens: I belong to *this* people because I oppose *that* one. Thus, the various clans occupying the island of Ireland developed a sense of Irish identity partly in common opposition to English (and Scottish) intrusion. And the English and Scots together developed a sense of British identity partly in common opposition to French Catholic monarchical absolutism and then French revolutionary republicanism. And the various American colonists developed a common sense of American identity, first in reaction to the cultural difference of Britons and then in opposition to what they perceived as British tyranny. Since nations are constituted by national consciousness, and since this consciousness is reactive, it follows that nations are contingent in origin.

Notwithstanding this, the fading of the original irritant need not cause the dissolution of common national consciousness, insofar as that consciousness has found institutional expression. For through institutions a people's peculiar linguistic grip on the world, customary incarnation of social values, and political ideals achieve a relatively stable state, which can survive the cooling of the original crucible. These institutions can be cultural and civil social, rather than political; and if political, they can enjoy

---

19. Fichte, *Addresses to the German Nation*, 135–36.
20. Barth, *Church Dogmatics*, III/4, 285–323.

varying degrees of autonomy. Not every nation is a nation-state; and not every nation-state has maximal sovereignty.

Take Scotland as an example. For almost three hundred years from 1707–1999 the Scottish nation expressed its self-consciousness primarily through the Church of Scotland and the Scottish legal system, both of whose jurisdictions covered the same defined territory. While retaining a measure of autonomy over local government (much of which operated through the church or "Kirk" well into the nineteenth century), the Scots had no autonomous control over economic, welfare, or foreign policy. Insofar as they elected representatives to the British parliament at Westminster, and insofar as their representatives succeeded in wielding influence there, they were able to exercise some control—but it was not autonomous. However, since the devolution of power by the British government to Scotland in 1999, and the creation of a Scottish parliament, the Scots now exercise a much greater degree of autonomy over the shape of life in the territory of Scotland. Nevertheless, this autonomy is limited: while they can participate in shaping and pursuing a British foreign policy, the Scots still cannot shape and pursue a simply Scottish one. The Scottish nation, therefore, enjoys statehood, but not of a fully sovereign kind.

Nations are contingent, evolving, and transitory phenomena. In that sense, they are artificial, not natural. And they are certainly not divine. However, in another sense they are natural, insofar as their customs and institutions incarnate a particular, perhaps distinctive grasp of the universal forms of flourishing suitable to human nature. Like families and churches and schools and supranational bodies, nations too can embody forms of human good, thus wielding moral authority and obliging our love. Moreover, when nations acquire full statehood, they come to possess maximal power to shape life within their borders so as to defend and promote goods. They also become centres of international agency, which bear responsibility for goods between nation-states, not least that of international order. Insofar as a nation-state has a record of virtuous action internally and externally, shaping life well within and without its borders, it deserves a measure of affection, loyalty, and gratitude as much as any beneficent family or global charity.

III. Babel's Benefit: The Good of Diversity

So far I have argued that considered reflection upon the Christian concept of the creatureliness of human being can justify a preference for benefitting near neighbors over distant ones, compatriots over foreigners; that it can also justify affection, loyalty, and gratitude toward those communities, customs, and institutions that mediate forms of human flourishing or human goods; and that a nation is one such community and set of customs and institutions. Now I want to contend that the creaturely quality of the human condition also implies that a diversity of communities, including nations, is a natural necessity that is also good.

Human communities, being creaturely, can only exist in particular times and places; and different geographical locations and historical experiences are bound to generate diverse communities. Human communities, being human, will all share some common characteristics; but experience of different places and histories is bound to generate differences in political constitutions, institutions, customs, received wisdom, and outlook. As a natural necessity, such diversity could be regarded simply as an unhappy feature of the human condition, providing as it does the occasion for inter-communal incomprehension and conflict, and therefore one to be transcended as soon as possible. But Christians, believing as they do in the unqualified goodness and wisdom of the divine Creator, should be disinclined to regard anything natural—whether created or following necessarily from it—as simply evil. Further, human experience confirms that diversity among peoples can be a source of value as well as of conflict. As postmodernists never tire of reminding us, there is beauty in difference. But to restrict this value simply to the aesthetic dimension would be to trivialize many of the differences that concern us here. For differences between constitutions, institutions, customs, wisdom, or outlook, if taken seriously, should provoke not merely wonder but reflective engagement. It should move each community to ask itself whether others do not order their social life better, or whether foreign wisdom should not correct, supplement, or complement its own. The value of communal (and so national) difference here is not just aesthetic, but intellectual and moral: it can enable human beings to learn from each other better ways of serving and promoting the human good. In other words, its justification is not just postmodernist, but liberal (in the style of J. S. Mill).

This argument that a Christian vision of things should affirm national diversity is supported by history. For, according to Adrian Hastings,

Christianity has been a vital factor in the historical development of national diversity through its habit of communicating its message by translating it into vernacular languages.[21] Since "a community . . . is essentially a creation of human communication,"[22] and since the writing down of a language tends to increase linguistic uniformity,[23] the movement of a vernacular from oral usage to the point where it is regularly employed for the production of a literature is a major cause of the development of national identity.[24] Therefore, by translating the Bible into vernacular languages, by developing vernacular liturgies and devotional literature, and by mediating these to the populace through an educated parish clergy, the Christian church has played a major part in the development of diverse nationalities.[25]

And there is good reason to suppose that this role has not simply been the accidental effect of a particular missionary strategy. After all, different missionary strategies are possible; and we must ask why Christianity chose the one that it did. It could, like Islam, have chosen to spread the Word by assimilation rather than translation. Muslims regard the Qur'an as divine in its Arabic, linguistic form as well as in its content, and the consequent cultural impact of Islam has been to Arabize, "to draw peoples into a single world community of language and government."[26] In contrast, Christians do not ascribe divinity to any particular language, and they thereby implicitly recognize that the Word of God is free to find (somewhat different) expression in every language.[27] Accordingly, in the New Testament story of the birth of the Christian church on the day of Pentecost, the disciples

21. Hastings, *The Construction of Nationhood*.
22. Ibid., 20.
23. Ibid., 19f.
24. Ibid., 12, 20, 31.
25. Ibid., 22, 24, 191–92. To take one example, the translation of the New Testament into Bulgarian in the mid-nineteenth century was a major factor in crystallizing a Bulgarian national identity. According to Mark Mazower (*The Balkans*, 99), "Religious changes did more than patriotic activism to shape an emerging Bulgarian consciousness. American Protestant missionaries translated the New Testament into a language Bulgarian peasants could understand, and thereby began to erode the dominance of Greek."
26. Ibid., 201. This statement needs to be qualified in that the traditional dogma of the untranslateability of the Qur'an has come under question as Islam has established itself in non-Arabic cultures.
27. Protestant fundamentalists, who believe the Bible to be inspired by God in the sense of being divinely dictated, come closest among Christians to the traditional Muslim view of the Qur'an; but not even they insist that the Sacred Scriptures should be read publicly only in Hebrew or Greek.

of Jesus "were all filled with the Holy Spirit and began to speak in other tongues," so that the multi-ethnic crowd who heard them "were bewildered, because each one heard them speaking in his own language."[28] Whereas the story of the tower of Babel in the Hebrew Scriptures presents linguistic diversity as a degeneration (caused by God's punishment of sin) from an original state when "the whole earth had one language,"[29] here the Spirit of God is presented as graciously accommodating Godself to it. This divine self-accommodation implies a respect for and affirmation of the historicality, and therefore diversity, of creaturely human being. Such affirmation is also implicit in the orthodox Christian doctrine of the divine incarnation, according to which God almighty became human in Jesus of Nazareth, and in becoming human became historical—that is, a *particular* man living in a *particular* time and place. According to the Christian story, it is characteristic of God to be willing to meet human creatures in the midst of their historicality and diversity. Although transcending time and space, God is not alien to them; in this case what is transcended is not repudiated and may be inhabited. The Christian theological affirmation of human diversity finds further confirmation in the orthodox doctrine of God as a Trinity. In Christian eyes, as in Jewish and Muslim ones, God is certainly one; but the divine unity is not simple. God is more like a community than a monad splendid in isolation. The divine Origin and Basis of the created world, then, is a unity that contains rather than abolishes difference—a unity *in* diversity, not *instead of* it.

In case my affirmation of national diversity should appear idiosyncratic, let me point out that it is a consistent characteristic of Anglican thought from at least the mid-nineteenth century to the present day. So, for example, in 1869 F. D. Maurice affirmed "the sanctity of national life";[30] distinguished a nation's reverence for its own language, laws, and government from a contempt for foreigners;[31] envisaged Christ's kingdom as "a kingdom for all nations" and not a "world-empire";[32] and argued that war is lawful only as "a struggle for Law against Force; for the life of a people as expressed in their laws, their language, their government, against any effort

---

28. Acts 2:4, 6.
29. Genesis 11.1–9.
30. Maurice, *Social Morality*, 183. These lectures were first published in 1869.
31. Ibid., 191.
32. Ibid., 180.

Loyalty and Limits

to impose on them a law, a language, a government which is not theirs."[33] Such views survived the First World War. In his 1928 Henry Scott Holland Memorial Lectures, William Temple affirmed the variety of nations against a non-national cosmopolitanism; and argued that a state has not only the right, but a duty, to defend itself against annihilation, because "each national community is a trustee for the world-wide community, to which it should bring treasures of its own; and to submit to political annihilation may be to defraud mankind of what it alone could have contributed to the general wealth of human experience."[34] A little later in his 1935-36 Gifford Lectures, Hensley Henson drew a sharp distinction between genuine patriotism, which is an extension of neighborly love, and "self-centred, vainglorious nationalism": "Patriotism pictures humanity as a composite of many distinctive national types, enriched with the various achievements of history. Nationalism dreams of a subject world, an empire of its own wherein all men serve its interests and minister to its magnificence."[35] Most recently, this affirmation of distinctive national life against global imperialism or cosmopolitanism has found expression in the thought of Oliver O'Donovan. In his *The Desire of the Nations: Rediscovering the Roots of Political Theology* (1986), O'Donovan invokes biblical authority in favour of an international order that is unified by universal law rather than by universal, imperial government, and which is constituted by a plurality of nations, each with their own cultural integrity.[36] Unlike empire, "[l]aw holds equal and independent subjects together without allowing one to master the other."[37]

IV. National Responsibility to Natural Law

Let us pause and review the route taken so far, before we take a further turn. On the ground of an understanding of human being as creaturely, I have argued that it might be preferable to benefit compatriots over foreigners, and that it is justifiable to feel affection, loyalty, and gratitude toward a nation whose customs and institutions have inducted us into created forms of human flourishing. I have also argued on the ground of the doctrines of

33. Ibid., 179.
34. Temple, *Christianity and the State*, 172, 156.
35. Henson, *Christian Morality*, 269.
36. O'Donovan, *The Desire of the Nations*, 70-73.
37. Ibid., 236.

creation, the incarnation of God, and the Trinity—as well as by appeal to the consistent witness over more than a century of at least one Christian tradition—that a diversity of nations is a natural phenomenon that generates certain benefits and should be affirmed. That is the rearward view. Now let us turn around again and move forward into different but complementary territory, in order to explore the matter of moral responsibility for the common good and the limitations this places on national loyalty.

Again, our theological point of departure is the doctrine of creation. As creatures, human beings are bound not only by time and space, but also by the requirements of the good that is proper to their created and universal nature. Service of the human good is what makes actions right, and failure of such service is what makes them wrong. This good is not just private, but common; the good of the human individual—the good of each human community or nation—is bound up with the good of others, both human and non-human. Acting rightly is important, then, partly because it respects or promotes the good of others in ways they deserve, and partly because in so doing agents maintain or promote their own good—and thereby help to make themselves fit for eternal life.

So human creatures are bound by an obligation to serve the common human good; but being creatures, their powers of service are limited. No human effort, individual or collective, has the power to secure the maximal good of all human beings (including the dead as well as the living), far less of non-human ones as well. Each of us must choose to do what he can, and what he may, to advance *certain* dimensions of the good of *some*, trusting divine providence to coordinate all our little contributions and guide their unpredictable effects to the benefit of the common good. Among those whom we choose to help, it would be right for us to include our benefactors; for gratitude requires it. This is the justification for special loyalties to such communities as one's family and nation.

But note: what one owes one's family or nation is not anything or everything, but specifically respect for and promotion of their good. Such loyalty, therefore, does not involve simply doing or giving whatever is demanded, whether by the state, the electoral majority, or even the people as a whole. Indeed, when what is demanded would appear to harm the community—for example, acquiescence in injustice perpetrated by the state against its own people or a foreign one, or by one section of the nation against another—genuine national loyalty requires that it be refused. True patriotism is not uncritical; and in extreme circumstances it might even involve participation in acts of treason—as it did in the case of Dietrich Bonhoeffer, whose love for Germany led him into conspiracy to kill Hitler.[38] National loyalty, as Christians should conceive it, shows itself basically in reminding the nation that it is accountable to God, at least in the sense of being obliged by the good given or created in human nature. By thus distinguishing between its object and God, such loyalty distances itself from the Romantic nationalism that absolutizes and divinizes the "Nation," making its unquestioning service the route to a quasi-immortality.

It is true, of course, that the Christian Bible contains and gives prominence to the concept of a people chosen by God to be the medium of salvation to the world; and it is also true that particular Christianized nations have periodically identified themselves as the chosen people, thereby pretending to accrue to themselves and their imperial, putatively civilizing, policies an exclusive divine authority. But, as I have already pointed out, the notion of the chosen people as referring to a particular nation strictly belongs to the Old Testament, not the New; and one of the main points on which early Christianity differentiated itself from Judaism was precisely its transnational character. Full participation in the Christian religion was no longer tied to worship in the Temple at Jerusalem, and was as open to Gentiles as to Jews; for, as St. Paul famously put it, "there is neither Jew nor Greek . . . for you are all one in Christ Jesus."[39] In early, emergent Christianity, the "people of God" came to refer, no longer to a particular nation (Israel), but to the universal church. Certainly, there have been many times when the church as an institution has become wedded to a particular ethnic culture or the instrument of a particular nation-state. There have been times when the church's *relative and conditional* affirmation of a particular culture or nation has lost its vital qualifiers. Nevertheless, in the light of what we have said above, we may judge that these are times when the church has betrayed its identity and failed in its calling. They are times when it has failed to maintain the distinction ironically attested by the Nazi judge, who, before condemning Helmuth James von Moltke to death, demanded of him, "From whom do you take your orders? From the Beyond or from Adolf Hitler?"[40] and they are times when it has failed to observe the original

---

38. For a fuller exploration of these themes in the light of Bonhoeffer's life and work, see Clements, *True Patriotism: Love of Country in Dialogue with the Witness of Dietrich Bonhoeffer*.

39. Gal 3:28.

40. Moltke, *Letters to Freya*, 409.

priority so succinctly affirmed in Sir Thomas More's declaration, moments before he was beheaded for refusing to endorse Henry VIII's assertion of royal supremacy over the English Church, that he would die "the King's good servant, but God's first."[41]

A properly Christian view, then, insists that every nation is equally accountable to God for its service of the human good. No nation may pretend to be God's chosen people in the strong sense of being the sole and permanent representative and agent of God's will on earth; no nation may claim such an identity with God. This relativization still permits each nation to consider itself chosen or called by God to contribute in its own peculiar way to the world's salvation; to play a special role—at once unique, essential, and limited—in promoting the universal human good. It allows members of a given nation to celebrate the achievements of the good that grace their own history and to take pride in the peculiar institutions and customs in which they have realized it. At the same time, it forces them to acknowledge that their nation's achievement is but one among many; and so to recognize, appreciate, and even learn from the distinctive contributions of others.

But more than this, each nation must realize, not only that other nations too have made valuable contributions to the realization of the common good of all things, but also that the achievement of the good in one nation is actually bound up with its achievement elsewhere. National loyalty, therefore, is properly extrovert. As Karl Barth put it:

> when we speak of home, motherland, and people, it is a matter of outlook, background, and origin. We thus refer to the initiation and beginning of a movement. It is a matter of being faithful to this beginning. But this is possible only if we execute the movement, and not as we make the place where we begin it a prison and stronghold. The movement leads us relentlessly, however, from the narrower sphere to a wider, from our own people to other human peoples.... The one who is really in his own people, among those near to him, is always on the way to those more distant, to other peoples.[42]

---

41. According to a contemporary report carried in the *Paris News Letter*. See Harpsfield, *The life and death of Sir Thomas Moore*, Appendix III, p. 266: "Apres les exhorta, et supplia tres instamment qu'ils priassent Dieu pour le Roy, affin qu'il luy voulsist donner bon conseil, protestant qu'il mouroit son bon serviteur et de Dieu premierement."

42. Barth, *Church Dogmatics*, III/4, 293-94.

Loyalty and Limits

The point here is not that we should grow *out of* national identity and loyalty and into a cosmopolitanism that, floating free of all particular attachments, lacks any real ones;[43] but rather that, in and through an ever-deepening care for the good of our own nation, we are drawn into caring for the good of foreigners. This point is poignantly captured by Yevgeni Yevtushenko in "Babii Yar," his poem about Russian anti-semitism:

> Oh my Russian people!
> I know you are internationalists to the core.
> But those with unclean hands
> have often made a jingle of your purest name.
> I know the goodness of my land . . .
> In my blood there is no Jewish blood.
> In their callous rage all anti-semites
> must hate me now as a Jew.
> For that reason I am a true Russian.[44]

Notwithstanding the tensions that may arise between national loyalty and more extensive ones, there is nevertheless an essential connection between them.

V. National Borders: Defending, Transgressing, Erecting

Christianity gives qualified affirmation to national loyalty and the nation, refusing to dismiss such things as the delusory products of false consciousness. It resists liberal cosmopolitanism and Marxist internationalism on the ground that human beings are not historically transcendent gods, but historically rooted and embedded creatures. Accordingly, it recognizes the need to control and limit cross-border mobility. Borders exist primarily to define the territory within which a people is free to develop its own way

---

43. Barth is right to suggest that such cosmopolitanism is not only undesirable, but impossible: "The command of God certainly does not require any man to be a cosmopolitan, quite apart from the fact that none of us can really manage to be so" (*Church Dogmatics*, III/4, 293). Here I differ from Miller ("Christian Attitudes," 27-28), who understands Barth's "overall impetus" to be "universalist," and interprets him as granting national identity and loyalty only "provisional" affirmation.

44. Yevtushenko, "Babii Yar," 103-4. "Babii Yar" is the name of a ravine on the outskirts of Kiev where at least 100,000 Jews were massacred in 1941. The massacre was carried out by German troops; but not without the tacit approval of many local Ukrainians, who shared in the long Russian tradition of anti-semitism.

of life as best it can. Unrestricted mobility would permit uncontrolled immigration that would naturally be experienced by natives as an invasion. Successful, peaceful immigration needs to be negotiated: immigrants must demonstrate a willingness to respect the ways of their native hosts and to a certain extent abide by them; natives must be given time to accommodate new residents and their foreignness.[45]

Further, the consensus that comprises the cohering identity of a nation needs to be more than merely constitutional; it also needs to be cultural. The reason for this is partly that, since a particular political constitution and its institutional components derive their particular meaning from the history of their development, fully to affirm that constitution involves understanding its history and owning its heroes. The second reason is that, while consensus over individual and group rights is necessary to prevent the outbreak of conflict, it cannot be secured or sustained without a constructive cultural *engagement* between groups that goes beyond standoffish respect and achieves a measure of mutual appreciation.

On the other hand, Christianity's qualification of its affirmation of nations means that it is alert to their historical mutability. While outgrowths of a natural love for human goods and of a consequent natural loyalty to their customary and institutional incarnations, particular nations are also human constructions whose culture and ethnic composition are always changing.[46] National myths of racial or ethnic or cultural purity, therefore, are immediately suspect; in which case, foreign ways and foreign immigrants can be regarded, not just as challenges or threats, but also as resources.

Christianity's view of the nation implies that its borders should be patrolled so as to control immigration, but that they should be open to foreign immigrants on certain conditions, and therefore that they should contain

---

45. I observe that two leading liberal-left thinkers in Britain—David Goodhart and Paul Collier—have recently broken ranks with multiculturalist orthodoxy, to argue in favour of controlled immigration for the sake of preserving a nation's cultural cohesion (Goodhart, *The British Dream*; Collier, *Exodus: How Migration is Changing our World*). I have already quoted Goodhart in note 1 above. Collier writes that his book is "a critique of the prevailing opinion among liberal thinkers, a group of which I am member, that modern Western societies should embrace a postnational future" (*Exodus*, 5). He goes on to argue that national identity "is enormously important as a force for equity" (ibid., 235), and that "[n]ations have not become obsolete. Reducing nationality to a mere legalism—a set of rights and obligations—would be the collective equivalent of autism: life lived with rules but without empathy" (ibid., 241).

46. Barth is admirably alert to this (*Church Dogmatics*, III/4, 300–302).

cultural diversity. The Christian view also implies that the autonomy a nation enjoys within its borders is not absolute. It does not have the right simply to do with its resources whatever it pleases, but only to manage them responsibly; and where it has resources surplus to its own needs, it has a duty to devote them to the good of others—by welcoming refugees, for example, or by donating aid to foreign countries.[47] This concept of a morally limited right to autonomy over material and social assets contradicts the libertarian view that one has an absolute right of disposal over whatever one has acquired legally; and it does so partly on the ground that all creaturely owners are also dependents and beneficiaries. How much we own is invariably due to benefactions and good fortune as well as to skill and entrepreneurial flair. Even where our property was genuinely virgin when we first came into possession of it, the fact that we had the power to discover it at all probably owed something to what we had inherited, and ultimately to what our ancestors had been given and the good fortune that had attended the development of their resources. As we have received, so should we give. Therefore, even *de iure*—*ius* being natural before it is contractual, given before it is made—national sovereignty is not absolute. Its exercise is subject to the moral claims of the common good, and when it fails to acknowledge those claims, other nations might have the moral right to intervene—if the requirements of prudence can be met (for example, if it seems that an intervention is likely to achieve what it intends and to do so without risking an escalating conflagration).

In the Christian view that I am commending here, national borders should be conditionally open and they may be transgressed, if national autonomy is being exercised irresponsibly. They may also be changed. Nations, as Christians should see them, are neither divine nor eternal, but human and historical. Investment in a nation is not—with all due respect to Fichte—the route to immortality; for that runs by way of service to the Creator and Sustainer of all things. As historical, nations are mutable. Therefore, the patriot should be willing to contemplate changes in his or her nation—whether in its constitution or even in its very definition—if that is what justice and prudence together require. It is not written in heaven that the United Kingdom should always encompass Scotland, nor the Canadian confederation Quebec, nor the Yugoslav federation Kosovo. Nor is it written that the United States of America must remain united, any

---

47. See Richard Miller's discussion of Thomas Aquinas' concept of private property in "Christian Attitudes," 19–25.

more than it was written that the Soviet Union should. Christianity properly precludes a simply conservative view of a nation's internal or external territorial boundaries, and withholds its support from political movements dedicated to preserve those boundaries at all costs.

On the other hand, Christians should be wary of demands for border-changes that issue from nationalist fervor fuelled by dishonest myths that idealize one's own nation and demonize or scapegoat another—myths that picture one's own simply as innocent victim and the other's simply as malicious oppressor. The Christian doctrine of the universal presence of sin means that we may not fondly imagine that the line dividing virtue from vice runs with reassuring neatness between our own people on the virtuous side and another people on the vicious one. The line between virtue and vice runs right down the middle of each human community, as it runs through the heart of every individual. Accordingly, no human may stand to another simply as righteous to unrighteous, and the wronged party always shares enough in common with the wrongdoer to owe them some compassion. Nationalist myths that say otherwise tend to exaggerate the injustice suffered, demand a radical and revolutionary remedy, totally discount any moral claims that the "enemy" might have, and brook no compromise.

For example, take Northern Ireland. It is true that Catholic nationalists there used to be seriously, albeit not atrociously, oppressed by Protestant unionists; and it is therefore reasonable for Catholics to be less than fully confident in British government and to seek protection under the Irish state. One way of securing this would be for the border between Northern Ireland and the Irish Republic to be completely erased, for the former to be incorporated into a "united" Ireland, and for British jurisdiction in the island of Ireland to be removed once and for all. This is what post-independence Irish nationalists have traditionally demanded.[48] The problem with this is that there is a substantial ethnic community in Northern Ireland whose national allegiance is strongly British, and who want to become subject to the Irish state about as much as nationalists want to remain subject to the British one. An alternative solution—and one embodied in the Good Friday Agreement reached between the British and Irish Governments and the political parties in Northern Ireland in April 1998—is to thin the border without erasing it. This involves setting up certain institutions

---

48. Before the Easter Rising of 1916 and the subsequent "War of Independence," most Irish nationalists sought "home rule" *within* the United Kingdom or at least *within* the British empire. In other words, they sought a measure of national autonomy that would not entirely remove British sovereignty.

that transcend the borders between Britain and Ireland, on the one hand compromising the substance of British sovereignty over Northern Ireland, while on the other hand maintaining the province's formal constitutional status as part of the United Kingdom. This reassures Irish nationalists by giving Dublin substantial influence over British government in Northern Ireland; and by creating bodies with specific areas of responsibility (say, for tourism), whose jurisdiction runs through the whole of the island of Ireland and is unhindered by the border. But it also reassures unionists by maintaining the border, eliciting Dublin's formal recognition of it,[49] limiting the jurisdiction of the cross-border bodies to specific areas of economic activity, and thereby securing Northern Ireland's place in the United Kingdom. One threat to this happy compromise, however, could come from the refusal of nationalists to regard it as a permanent settlement and their insistence on viewing it as merely a step on the road to the ultimate goal of the political unification of the whole of the island of Ireland under an Irish state. Such an insistence would be fuelled by a traditional resentment of all things British and unionist—a resentment that is blind to the considerable progress in remedying the injustices suffered by Catholics that British governments are widely acknowledged to have made since the 1970s, and which doggedly refuses to acknowledge the right of unionists to maintain their British allegiance for ever.

As I see it, therefore, a Christian vision of things militates against the idealization of the self and the demonization of the other that together stifle sympathy and issue in a bitter, dogmatic nationalism that brooks no compromise in its determination to erase a national boundary. The same vision also militates against a nationalism that, enthralled by an exaggerated sense of its own victimhood, a correlative inclination to transfer its own sins onto a foreign scapegoat, and a consequent lust for independence, refuses all compromise in its determination to erect a national boundary.

Sometimes, of course, there are good reasons for a nation to seek expression in its own fully sovereign state—and so to secede from the larger multinational or imperial whole, of which it is a part. The strongest reason is seriously unjust oppression suffered by a national minority, which the majority consistently refuses to remedy. The Dutch in the mid-sixteenth century, for example, had just cause to secede from the Spanish empire,

---

49. As part of the Agreement, the Irish Government committed itself to amend Articles 2 and 3 of the Irish constitution, so as to relinquish the Irish state's claim to the territory of Northern Ireland.

which was committed to the violent suppression of the Protestant religion; and the Kosovars in the late twentieth century had just cause to secede from the rump of the Serbian-dominated Yugoslav federation, which was engaged in the ruthless and indiscriminate ethnic cleansing of Muslims. A less strong but still sufficient reason for seeking greater autonomy (if not outright separation) is the denial to a minority of proportionate representation or the chronic overruling or neglect of its important and legitimate interests. Thus the Irish in the nineteenth century were justified, arguably, in using their representation in the imperial parliament at Westminster to press for a measure of "home rule" in Dublin, so that Irish concerns could receive the attention that they deserved.

Sometimes, then, a nationalist movement is right to demand greater autonomy, even to the point of full sovereignty. But, equally, sometimes it is wrong. Take, for example, the Scottish National Party's campaign for independence from the United Kingdom in the run-up to the referendum of 2014. Were it the case that membership of the United Kingdom's multinational state had inflicted some grave and chronic injustice on the Scottish people, for which remedy had long been sought but never found, then the case for secession would have been cogent. Perhaps the Scots were underrepresented at Westminster. Perhaps their legitimate concerns were neglected and their needs unfairly met. Perhaps their culture was suppressed. But none of this was so. Since the Scottish parliament came into being in 1999, the Scots had enjoyed representation both in Edinburgh and in London. Indeed, Scottish Members of (the Westminster) Parliament could vote on matters concerning other parts of the U.K. (England, Wales, and Northern Ireland), whereas the representatives of those other parts could not vote on matters devolved to Edinburgh. In the U.K. the Scots received more public spending per capita than the English, and whatever it was that struck visitors to Edinburgh and Glasgow it was not a signal lack of cultural vitality.

How, then, did the S.N.P. justify its campaign for independence? Its strongest card was the argument that the Scots prefer a left-of-centre, social democratic polity with a more generous welfare state, whereas, judging by its propensity to elect Conservative governments, the centre of gravity of the English electorate is markedly further to the right and more favourable to the free market. If this had been true, it would have been an argument for greater Scottish autonomy and a further devolution of powers from Westminster to Edinburgh, although not necessarily for outright secession

Loyalty and Limits

from the United Kingdom. As it happens, however, the claims of nationalist politicians did not match the evidence of the social scientific data. According to analysis of the British Social Attitudes (B.S.A.) survey of 2010:

> it seems that Scotland is not so different after all. Scotland is somewhat more social democratic than England. However, for the most part the difference is one of degree rather than of kind—and is no larger now than it was a decade ago. Moreover, Scotland appears to have experienced something of a drift away from a social democratic outlook during the course of the past decade, in tandem with public opinion in England.[50]

From this the authors conclude that "the task of accommodating the policy preferences of people in both England and in Scotland within the framework of the Union is no more difficult now than it was when devolution was first introduced."[51]

Beyond the false assertion of a major difference in political preferences between Scotland and England, the S.N.P.'s platform consisted of claims that membership of the U.K. somehow inhibits Scotland's economic growth and that the standard of living in an independent Scotland would be higher. These claims were contingent on a number of variable and (in the crucial matter of the price of oil) volatile factors. They were also necessarily speculative and fiercely contested. The debate went back and forth and seemed quite finely balanced. The very least that can be said is that it was not at all certain that independence would make the Scots better off economically, and that there was little reason to suppose that it would make them dramatically so.

What is most striking about the S.N.P.'s case was its vagueness and ad hoc nature. The goal of independence did not seem to be the logical conclusion of a rigorous analysis of particular problems afflicting the Scottish people. Rather, it seemed an article of faith in search of a rationale. This is certainly the impression given by reading David Torrance's recent biography of Alex Salmond, the S.N.P's charismatic leader, which identifies no moment of intellectual conversion, when Scottish independence was revealed as the solution to any particular problem.[52] As an early colleague observed of Salmond, "when you went through all the arguments you were

---

50. Curtice and Ormston, "On the Road to Divergence? Trends in Public Opinion in Scotland and England," 33–34. While published in 2012, the data was collected in 2010.
51. Ibid., 34.
52. David Torrance, *Salmond against the Odds*.

left with the impression that he didn't know if Scotland would be better or worse off as an independent country. All that mattered was that Scots should rule themselves."[53]

So what is it that filled the sails of the separatists? In part, a sense of Scottish victimhood, which can find little foothold in actual history, together with a correlative scapegoating of the *Sassenach*.[54] In part, a modern and adolescent faith in the fetish of independence. And in part—judging by the barely visible connection between analysis and aspiration—a desire to escape the hard graft of daily politics into the uplift of a grander, purer, freer vision of things.[55] Vision is good, of course, for, as we are told, the people perish without it. But vision needs to be born of a sober and moral reckoning with reality. Otherwise, it is just wishful thinking kept afloat on a mixture of self-pity, resentment, and recklessness, and destined for disillusion.

Nationalist calls for independence and erecting fresh borders are not self-justifying. And Christians, with their sensitivity to the creaturely interdependence of human individuals and communities, and with their conviction that God, the Origin and Basis of things, comprises a unity-in-diversity rather than the isolated and alienated unity of absolute

---

53. Torrance, *Salmond*, 88.

54. *Sassenach* is the Gaelic word for "Saxon" or "English"—probably the only Gaelic word that most Scots ever learn. I write from experience. Ever since my childhood in Galloway and Ayrshire, I have been aware of the background noise of Scottish resentment of the *Sassenach*. Usually, when I was growing up, it was at least half-jocular. Still, notwithstanding my English mother and my English-educated father, it managed to infect even me. Thus in 1965 at the age of ten, when I first saw Peter Watkins' classic television docudrama about the 1746 battle of Culloden (in which the last Jacobite rebellion was defeated), I was already programmed to *mis*read it as yet another defeat suffered by the poor Scots at the hands of the ruthless English. Having watched *Culloden* again more recently and having observed how clearly it presents the conflict more as a Scottish civil war than an English-versus-Scots one—a war in which my own people, the Lowland Scots, wore redcoats, not kilts—I can now see how much anti-English prejudice it took to make that juvenile misreading. For sure, my particular experience of Scottish scapegoating was almost fifty years ago, and, if Alex Salmond is to be believed, then Scottish nationalism has since matured into being pro-Scottish rather than anti-English. That may well be his party's official position, but recent reports suggest that it does not accurately reflect sentiment on the street. Moreover, I have observed how Salmond resorted to the levers of resentment—to stereotypes of English bullying and Scottish victimhood—for example, during his visit to Dublin in 2012, when he dared to align Scotland with Ireland as common victims of English colonialism (Watt, "Scottish Independence Referendum: Salmond Attacks UK's 'Bullying Tactics'").

55. Here, I have in mind Jim Gallagher's characteristically pithy insight, not yet committed to print, that, in the S.N.P.'s case, "nationalism is a substitute for politics."

self-sufficiency, should be sceptical of cries for it. They should interrogate the demand closely, asking whether it will bring real and substantial benefits to the people as a whole—and not just, say, provide the local political class with a bigger stage to strut upon.

VI. Conclusion

In this opening chapter I have argued for the moral legitimacy of a limited national loyalty and of a measure of national autonomy. Nations are not divine; they rise and fall, come and go. In one sense they are cultural constructs and therefore artificial. In another sense, however, nations are natural, insofar as they incarnate universal human goods in their customs and institutions, and since it is natural for human beings to love those goods and to be grateful to those communities that make them present. If a nation has customs and institutions that embody goods—and perhaps also distinctive insight into their nature and practical implications—it is right that it should defend them, the cultural hinterland that makes them intelligible, and the autonomy that makes their authentic development possible. Since unlimited immigration can pose a threat to national customs, institutions, and culture that are morally valuable, borders should be policed.

This is not a view with which multiculturalist orthodoxy sits easily. In over-reaction against crude notions of racial superiority, multiculturalism tends to assert the moral equality of all cultures. Consequently, it refuses to recognize the legitimacy of defending the integrity of a national culture and its continued dominance over sub-cultures. In this it is supported by the prevailing tradition of liberal political theory, which holds that a liberal state should be neutral with regard to rival versions of the good life. To this—and to arguing against it—I now turn.

2

Unity In Diversity? The English Case

I: The Need for Humanist Unity in Liberal Diversity

Within limits, a nation should be open to incorporating foreigners and with them elements of their foreignness: it should admit and contain a measure of cultural diversity. Strictly speaking, the word "should" here is redundant, since nations invariably *do* contain such diversity. Ethnic and cultural purity and homogeneity might be a property of families and villages—although even there the clash of differences has been known—but it is certainly not the property of anything as large and complex as a nation and *a fortiori* a nation-state. Still, if nations and nation-states cannot be obliged to become what they already are, they can be obliged to *acknowledge* what they already are, and not to use the myth of original purity as a justification for the scapegoating of a particular group.

Cultural diversity within a nation is a fact; it is also, within limits, a good, leavening the cultural status quo with fresh, perhaps valuable perspectives and practices. But should cultural diversity extend to religious diversity? There are good Christian grounds for supposing that it should. Even if Christians believe that they have a better grasp of certain vital truths than others (as others no doubt believe that they have a better grasp than Christians), it does not follow from this that non-Christians are absolutely or radically wrong. Christians believe that the Spirit of the Christ-like God is universally present to all creatures; so they should expect that God is somewhat known beyond the reaches of the Christian church. Add to this the Protestant doctrine of the church as a body that is still *learning* to be faithful—as at once righteous and sinful—and Christians come to be seen as those who have yet more to learn, and who might conceivably do so from non-Christians. Then, combining these theological considerations with the empirical observation (and Christians should not be averse to learning from experience) that the modern era has shown that religious uniformity is not necessary for a moral consensus sufficient to ensure social stability, we arrive at the conclusion that a nation should be willing to tolerate religious diversity within its borders.

Nevertheless, cultural and religious diversity needs to be contained and disciplined by the nation's public affirmation of a particular worldview. The reason for this is that cultural nature, like physical nature, abhors a vacuum. So if a national community does not actively commit itself to a view of reality that includes a high estimation of human dignity and freedom, then an alternative, non-humanist view will come to prevail, first in popular assumptions and then in law and policy.

To illustrate this point, let me refer to the London suicide-bombings of 7 July 2005. The bombers, I suggest, were not wholly wrong. They were wrong in what they did, of course, but they were not wholly wrong in why they did it. Their motives were mixed, but among them was moral disgust— disgust at the obsession with the consumption of material goods, which, they felt, characterized the culture enveloping them. In the video-tape that he left behind their leader, Mohammad Sidique Khan, was scathing about the British media's administering materialism to the masses, asserting that "*our* driving agenda doesn't come from tangible commodities that this world has to offer."[1] Moreover, maybe it was no coincidence that, before he turned politically radical, Khan was involved in helping young Asian drug addicts kick their habit;[2] maybe the road to cathartic violence went through his direct experience of the degrading symptoms of a popular culture that much prefers being out of one's mind to being in it.

Lest my reading of the bombers' motives should seem like an expression of the predictable pessimism of one sinking into the natural conservatism of middle-age, I appeal to a remarkable article published in *The Guardian*, a left-wing newspaper, in 2006. There the card-carrying liberal, Timothy Garton Ash, wrote:

> Britain now has one of the most libertine societies in Europe. Particularly among younger Brits in urban areas, which is where most

1. Cowell, "Al Jazeera Video Links London Bombings to Al Qaeda."
2. Malik, "My Brother the Bomber," 31.

British Muslims live, we drink more alcohol faster, sleep around more, live less in long-lasting, two parent families, and worship less, than almost anyone in the world. It's clear from what young British Muslims themselves say that part of their reaction is against this kind of secular, hedonistic, anomic lifestyle. . . . The idea that these young British Muslims might actually be putting their fingers on some things that are wrong with our modern, progressive, liberal, secular society . . . hardly feature[s] in everyday progressive discourse. But [it] should.[3]

Garton Ash does not give us an exact diagnosis of what he thinks is wrong with contemporary liberal society in Britain, maybe because its implications are too troubling to excavate. So I shall venture where he fears, or at least fails, to tread. What Garton Ash directly implies is that at least in parts of our liberal society, the individual's exercise of freedom often amounts to the voluntary selling of the self into the slavery of addiction, which not only degrades the agent but damages the society to which he belongs. The indirect implication of this, which is troubling for a certain, modern kind of liberal, is that a liberal society really cannot afford to limit itself to affirming the freedom of individuals to pursue whatever vision of life they happen to fancy. They cannot afford it, not only because it allows individual human beings to degrade themselves, but also because this causes wider social damage, which includes the degeneration of habits of self-control, without which individuals lack the power to respect the freedom of others. In other words, a libertarian version of liberal society is actually self-subverting.

This diagnosis of the ills of liberal society as we actually have it points to a fundamental error in modern liberal thinking. This consists in its deference to the persistent fantasy of Enlightenment philosophers that human beings are rational individuals, who are fully aware of their own best interests and are perfectly capable of deciding for themselves how these should be served. However, reflection on twentieth-century history in particular, if not on human life as experienced in general, furnishes ample evidence that human beings are disturbingly susceptible to being spell-bound and driven by self-destructive passions. Whether or not he is responsible for the Christian church's tendency to equate original sin with concupiscence, St. Augustine was not wrong, I think, to use (male) sexual desire as a prime example of the relative fatedness of human existence—of the extent to

3. Garton Ash, "What Young British Muslims Say Can Be Shocking—Some of It Is Also True," 25.

which human beings are considerably, if not absolutely, driven by physical, psychic, and social forces of which they have little understanding, and over which they have even less control.

Rationalist overestimation is the basic theoretical, anthropological error of modern liberalism; and it issues, ironically, in practical degradation. This is because the fantasy of rationally autonomous individuals serves to justify a "free market," where commercial interests are left at complete liberty to make money out of exciting and exploiting human passions. (After all, any one who does not want to consume online pornography is "free" to switch it off, isn't he?) In practice, then, rationalist overestimation results in consumerist degradation, where individuals are abandoned to the tender mercies of commercial exploitation, and encouraged hourly to satisfy exaggerated appetites. (After all, we're *worth* it.) However, according to a Christian view—and indeed according to any humanism worth the name—human beings are properly more than their hedonic appetites and aversions. They yearn—and are called—to invest themselves in intrinsically worthwhile things that will endow their passing lives with permanent meaning. Therefore, in a consumerist liberal culture such as ours, where specifically human aspirations tend to be trampled underfoot in the stampede for pleasure (or anaesthesia), one should expect humanity to rebel, and given a supporting ill wind, one would fear that rebellion might turn radical and even violent.

This speculative fear is given empirical corroboration by an event in the career of another radical Islamist. In 1993, Ed Husain was spearheading a campaign to "Islamize" public space in London's Tower Hamlets College—by holding public prayers, plastering the walls with Islamist posters, and encouraging women to wear the hijab. The college authorities grew alarmed and considered how best to combat the growing influence of Muslim radicalism. According to their best lights, they decided to try and divert students by holding raves and discos. The result was telling. As Husain recounts it,

> In early 1993, a thirty-minute video was handed in to me about the war in Bosnia, the ethnic cleansing of Muslims in the Balkans. I watched it in horror and then decided that it must be shown to our students to raise money for Bosnian Muslims.
>
> On Wednesday afternoon we booked a lecture theatre under the title of "The Killing Fields of Bosnia." . . . That same Wednesday afternoon the youth workers at college organized their second disco. . . . The Islamic society offered a video on the killing of

> Muslims by Christians. The youth workers offered dance, drugs, and delight. To our astonishment the lecture theatre was packed. The students had voted with their feet.[4]

Radical Islamism had dignified the students with moral seriousness. The college authorities, on the other hand, had nothing either humanly or morally serious to offer as an alternative. No doubt acting on what passes for liberal common sense, they had dramatically underestimated the humanity of their students. Consequently, their ability to counter the growing appeal of a humanly dignifying political radicalism was hamstrung.

Cultural nature abhors a vacuum. The affirmation of individual freedom alone merely clears space for the self-assertion and exploitation of human passions. So in addition to bare freedom, we need some vision of what a dignified exercise of it looks like. We need a substantially *humanist* liberalism. We need it as the prevailing cultural context in which laws and policies are made, and in which individuals exercise a responsible freedom, not an arbitrary one. And if that is what we as a national society need, then that is what our national institutions and public rites should affirm. That is, we need a certain humanism to be established by the national authorities or by the state as a public orthodoxy

II. From Humanist to Christian Establishment

Thus far I have argued that the establishment of humanism of some kind is important for the health—indeed the survival—of liberal society. Now I am going to argue that, in the case of the nation-state of England, the kind of humanism that should be established is Christian, and specifically Anglican.[5]

Since "establishment" can mean all manner of things—as a survey of European, indeed British, arrangements would quickly reveal[6]—let me make clear right at the beginning what I have in mind. First there is the Coronation Service, in which the head of state, kneeling, receives authorization from above, not from below. Contrary to the populist orthodoxy

---

4. Husain, *The Islamist*, 63, 74.

5. I argue only for the retention of the Anglican establishment in England. The Anglican church has never been established in Scotland; and it was disestablished in Ireland in 1869 and in Wales in 1920.

6. For an account of different forms of religious establishment in Europe, see Morris, ed., *Church and State in 21st Century Britain*.

that prevails among us, the moral legitimacy of government issues primarily from its faithfulness to the *given* principles of justice, and *not* from its reflection of popular will—as the fate of the Weimar Republic in the early 1930s should have taught us. In an era that finds it hard to think of political legitimacy except in terms of popular election, and which is therefore inclined to collapse a healthily mixed constitution into its democratic element, the Coronation Service makes an important and dramatic cautionary statement—and in our circumstances, a prophetic one.

Second is the affirmation by the head of state of the established church through the monarch's special association with it. While the specific disqualification of Roman Catholics from succeeding to the throne should be removed, the requirement of communion with the Church of England should remain. If the Roman Catholic church chooses to continue to prohibit its members from such communion, then that is a problem for Rome.

Third comes the sitting of Anglican bishops in the Upper House of Parliament. An Upper House ought to give the U.K. an "aristocracy" of expertise and experience, perchance wisdom, and not a mirror-image of the Lower House. Therefore its composition ought to guarantee the representation of civil society in all its variety—including the Church of England. Since direct elections cannot guarantee such representation, appointments will be necessary.[7]

The fourth thing that I have in mind when I talk about establishment is the Church of England's privileged position in state education.

These, then, are the constitutional, institutional, and ritual manifestations of Anglican Christian establishment that I want to defend and recommend. Against it there are two main arguments, both of them moral, one emanating from secularists and the other from within the Christian churches themselves. I shall deal with the latter first and briefly, since I do not think it cogent.

---

7. Russell, *Reforming the House of Lords*, 304, 318. Russell's concern here is with securing the presence of members of the House of Lords who are independent of political party discipline, including representatives of fields of expertise or of civil society. It is true that support in the House of Commons for the recommendation by the Wakeham Commission (2000) of a predominantly appointed—rather than elected—Upper House has waned; but, given what is at stake, I see no reason simply to go with the flow. It is also true that, if seats in the Upper House were opened up to representatives of non-Anglican religious communities, it might be difficult to agree on a formula for distribution that would keep everyone's nose entirely in joint (ibid., 330–31). But since when in politics was there ever an agreement that made everyone entirely happy? Frustration is a routine feature of political life, and tolerating it is a definitive feature of liberal political mores.

III. Answering the Christian Objection

The main Christian objection to establishment is that it corrupts the church, constraining its freedom to speak the truth to power. To this I would say, again, that "establishment" can mean all manner of things. Maybe in the past certain forms of it have spelled the Babylonian—or the Constantinian—captivity of the church, but I cannot see that it does so now. Establishment did not prevent the Church of England from making head-on criticism of the Thatcher Government in *Faith in the City* in 1985. Nor did it prevent the Archbishop of Canterbury (Rowan Williams) from publicly dissenting from Prime Minister Blair's decision to go to war against Iraq in 2003. Nor did it stop him from warning the current Coalition Government against using the "Big Society" as a fig-leaf for dismantling welfare provision.

Besides, the tying of its prophetic tongue is only one situation that the church should strive to avoid. Another is following an uncharitable and moralistic media into a self-flattering cynicism about those who bear responsibility for governing. With regard to the latter, establishment in the form of episcopal participation in the work of the House of Lords helps to keep at least one major civil social body sensitive to the difficulties and complexities of the necessary tasks of government. And this is important when too many leaders in the churches are inclined by the liberal *Zeitgeist* in general, and Liberation Theology in particular, to take a relentlessly critical view of the state, and to assume that a Christian voice has only one, prophetic register. Or, rather, to assume that prophecy always comes from the Left.[8]

IV. Answering the Secularist Objection via the Late Rawls

So much for criticism of establishment from within the churches themselves. Much more considerable, in my opinion, is the secularist critique. In a nutshell, this is that since we now live in a liberal, plural society, it is

---

8. In his critique of an earlier expression of my argument here, Theo Hobson ("Establishment and Liberalism: A Response to Nigel Biggar") judged that my dismissal in short order of "the Christian objection" to the establishment of religion had only succeeded in raising and levelling a straw man, and had entirely failed to engage with his own, more formidable position. Subsequently I examined his position, but did not find it cogent ("A Reply to Theo Hobson").

unfair for any one religion to be privileged; and that public institutions and rituals should therefore be neutral with regard to rival views of the world.

My response to this takes its cue from an unlikely quarter: namely, the thought of the pre-eminent theorist of liberal politics in recent times, the late John Rawls. Rawls's later work echoes many of the concerns about liberal society that I have already expressed. It is motivated by awareness that liberal values and the larger views that support them are not universally held, and that a liberal ethos is therefore contested and vulnerable. There will always be views that would suppress it—what he calls "unreasonable" comprehensive doctrines—and there is no guarantee that these will not prevail,[9] as they did in the case of the Weimar Republic.[10] The virtues of tolerance, of being ready to meet others halfway, of reasonableness, and of fairness comprise political capital that can depreciate and constantly needs to be renewed.[11] Consequently, Rawls tells us, "the problem of stability has been on our minds from the outset."[12]

It seems, then, that a liberal point of view is *not* neutral. It is not a view from nowhere. Liberal space is not indefinite. It is bounded by certain moral convictions, which are expressive of a certain understanding of human beings. Some worldviews will not support a liberal ethos; and some will actually corrode it. Therefore, if a liberal ethos is to survive, supportive views have to be fostered by public institutions and corrosive ones (somehow) suppressed: "The principles of any reasonable political conception," writes Rawls, "must impose restrictions on permissible comprehensive views, and the basic institutions those principles require inevitably encourage some ways of life and discourage others, or even exclude them altogether."[13]

(For the sake of clarity, let me pause here for a moment to bring to the surface something that has been implicit in what I have said so far: namely, that there are importantly different kinds of liberalism and different kinds of liberal ethos. Some, like Rawls's, are humanist, in that they presuppose a high notion of objective human dignity. The libertarian version I mentioned earlier is not humanist, I think, in that its logic collapses dignity into individual autonomy and ends up affirming consensual cannibalism of the

9. Rawls, *Political Liberalism*, 65. See also ibid., 126.
10. Ibid., lxi–lxii.
11. Ibid., 157 and n.23.
12. Ibid., 141.
13. Ibid., 195.

kind that Armin Meiwes and his willing victim practiced ten years ago in Germany.[14])

Rawls believes that a liberal view of human being and liberal values can find, and needs to find, support in a limited plurality of larger worldviews—what he calls "reasonable" comprehensive doctrines. Among these are his own secular Kantianism, but also certain versions of Christianity and, indeed, of Islam. So unlike militantly secularist liberals, he sees in certain kinds of religion, not enemies, but important allies. Nevertheless, he believes that public discourse—the discourse of parliament and the law courts, and perhaps also of public rituals—should not involve religious references, but should be conducted in terms of "public reason." Public reason comprises the set of liberal moral values and such anthropological tenets as are necessary to make sense of it, upon which various "reasonable" comprehensive doctrines converge. That is to say, it comprises the "overlapping [moral and anthropological] consensus," which he believes can be made to float free of the various larger theological and metaphysical views that sustain it.

Here I part company with Rawls.[15] While Kantian humanists and Christian humanists and Muslim humanists all affirm the liberal humanist value of human dignity, they do so in ways that are sometimes significantly different. Their common affirmation of human dignity does not prevent disagreement over, for example, how human fetuses should be treated or whether human beings should be permitted to control their dying by committing suicide. And these disagreements—these differences in interpretation—can be traced back into their deeper religious and philosophical worldviews. Public reason, therefore, is not entirely common. It is not neu-

14. In 2001 Armin Meiwes advertised on the internet for a well-built male prepared to be slaughtered and consumed. Out of over 800 respondents he eventually selected a forty-three-year-old, whom he met and took to his home in Rotenburg, Germany; and there, apparently with the victim's consent, he dismembered, killed, and ate him. In 2004 Meiwes was convicted of manslaughter; but in 2006, following a retrial, he was convicted of murder. The fact that Meiwes was judged guilty of a crime at all was only because German law had not endorsed a libertarian concept of autonomy. It had not endorsed the principle that individuals are the sole arbiters of the worth of their own lives, and of how and when they should end. Under German law (as under other Western legal systems), it is possible for someone to be guilty of treating their own lives too cheaply—even if they do so of their own free will—because the law is committed to an objective view of the worth of human life by which the decisions of individuals can be judged and contradicted.

15. For a fuller explanation of this point, see Biggar, "Not Translation, but Conversation: Theology in Public Debate about Euthanasia," esp. 178, 183–84.

tral. It does not float free of the larger comprehensive humanist doctrines that support it. On the contrary, these larger doctrines give rise to significant disagreements within the common terms of public reason. Rawls himself implicitly recognized this, at least on the margins of his thought, where he acknowledged that public reason involves radical controversy as well as consensus. Why else would we sometimes need to have recourse, as Rawls acknowledges we do, to decision by majority vote?

So, liberal humanist space is not indefinite. Nor should it be taken for granted, for it is under threat from a variety of anti-humanisms. Liberal public institutions that would survive, then, cannot afford to take a neutral position on ethics and anthropology. So far, so Rawlsian. Beyond Rawls, I propose that public institutions cannot afford to be neutral about which larger views of the world dominate public culture, since some of these are positively subversive of liberal ethics and anthropology. Public institutions that wish to be and remain liberal, therefore, must foster worldviews that commend the virtues necessary for liberal public discourse to flourish. They need to do this because, as Rawls rightly observed, there are illiberal barbarians inside the gates; and within living memory their number has been known to grow to democratically dominant proportions.

V. The Anglican Christian Option

There is an obvious problem, however, because, as Rawls also rightly observed, there is more than one humanist worldview that supports a liberal ethos. Presumably, a single set of public institutions and rituals cannot simultaneously affirm a variety of worldviews without sounding impossibly dissonant and incoherent. Rawls's solution was to argue that they should affirm only the overlapping consensus—whose content is mainly ethical and thinly anthropological—while keeping silent about any of the thicker metaphysical hinterlands. I have explained why I doubt that it is either possible or desirable for public reason to keep silence in this way. So if liberal public institutions and rituals cannot limit their affirmation simply to a common ethic, they must choose one supportive humanist worldview to represent.

So one must be chosen; but which? One candidate for public comprehensive doctrine is an atheist version of Kantianism, although this would need to become significantly less dogmatically secularist toward religious believers than French republicanism, if it were to be genuinely liberal.

Alternatively, liberal institutions could choose an ecumenical monotheism, as the U.S. Constitution permits and American governments have in fact chosen.[16] Or they could choose Trinitarian Christianity, as has the Republic of Ireland.[17] Or they could choose Anglican Christianity, as in England.

As an expression of orthodox Christianity, Anglicanism is structurally humanist in its creedal affirmation of the special dignity of human being made in the image of God—a dignity intensified by God's assumption of human flesh in the Incarnation. According to this high vision, human beings are not merely the random result of the blind operation of physical forces, nor their activity simply determined by genes or chemistry, nor their asserted significance just so much desperate whistling in the enveloping cosmic dark. No, in Christian eyes humans are the creatures of a benevolent divine intelligence, which has striven through natural evolution to bring about individuals who flourish in freely understanding and investing themselves in the truth about the world's good.

In such a vision, there is truth—be it sometimes complex and internally plural—to be understood: as the creation of the one wise God, the world possesses a given rationality that is there for rational beings to grasp. Since human beings are not only rational but finite and fallible, and since

---

16. The claim that American governments have established an ecumenical monotheism, notwithstanding the U.S. Constitution's forbidding federal and state governments from establishing the Christian church in general or any Christian church in particular, might surprise. The claim is Michael Perry's (*Under God?* 124–26), although he does not use the word "established." In support of this view he cites the theological references made by the Declaration of Independence, by Abraham Lincoln in his Gettysburg and Second Inaugural Addresses, by the Pledge of Allegiance, by the motto inscribed on U.S. coins and paper currency, by the prayers that attend the opening of sessions of state and federal legislatures, and by the invocation that precedes the business of the Supreme Court. Perry's view, of course, is controversial; but he is nevertheless a recognized authority on U.S. constitutional law.

17. The secularist narrative assumes that a republican constitution, in which no religion is established by the state, is requisite for a liberal society; and that a monarchical constitution, in which a particular religion is established, is essentially inimical to it. The histories of England and Ireland in the twentieth century tell a very different tale. Notwithstanding its formal separation of church and state, the Irish Constitution as adopted in 1937 gave special recognition to the Roman Catholic Church as "the guardian of the faith professed by the majority of the citizens." This statement was removed in 1972; but the Preamble to the Constitution still begins, "In the name of the Most Holy Trinity, from Whom is all authority and to Whom, as our final end, all actions both of men and States must be referred, We, the people of Ireland . . ." Further, Article 44 of the present Constitution starts by acknowledging "that the homage of public worship is due to Almighty God." See Cranmer, Lucas, and Morris, *Church and State*, 107.

they are made to flourish in society, their reasoning needs to be social: they need to reason *together*. Conversation, therefore, is an important social endeavour. It is not properly an occasion for the egotistical display of wit, for the scoring of clever points, for the assertion of superior rhetorical power, or for the domination of the weak by the strong. It is rather about the common searching out of the truth, and common deference to its authority.

Believing as it does in the (complex) unity and rationality of things, Christian humanism endows human conversation with a serious moral significance. It also has the resources to grace it with generous—and in that sense, "liberal"—virtues: openness to being taught and corrected, since it sees humans as finite and fallible; readiness to confess conversational dishonesty, since it also sees them as sinners; respect for others as potential speakers of the truth, since it regards everyone as a potential medium of God's word; tolerance of strange and unwelcome views, since finitude and fallibility preclude the identity of the familiar and the true; patience with frustrations in understanding, since truth is as much self-revealing as grasped, and since faith sustains the hope that what is now seen through a glass darkly shall yet be seen face to face; and forgiveness as a reaction to conversational injustice, since all victims are perpetrators too.

Surely, however, this account of Christianity and its Anglican expression is, as one anti-establishmentarian critic of an early expression of this argument put it, "a tad idealistic." How does their vaunted liberal humanism square with Christianity's actual history of authoritarianism and repression? And how does it square with the Church of England's record of persecuting Roman Catholics and nonconformists, with its ownership of slaves in the West Indies, with its grudging admission of women to the priesthood and episcopacy, and with its persistent exclusion from these of practicing homosexuals?

The first thing to say in defence is that *no* society can avoid asserting the authority of an orthodoxy against its heterodoxies, if necessary by means of coercive law. As we saw above, even John Rawls admitted as much of liberal societies; and as we shall see below, what Rawls admits, Martha Nussbaum unwittingly corroborates. "Liberal" is a relative term. Only totalitarian societies are simply illiberal; others are more or less liberal. Even medieval Christendom—now a secularist byword for violent, authoritarian repression—allowed public space for disagreement and tolerated the expression of controversial views. If that were not so, then there would have been no scholastic disputations in the universities. The difference between pre-modern Christian societies and contemporary liberal ones is a matter of degree, not kind. Modern liberal societies have their heretics too: sexists, racists, and homophobes, of course, but now also public critics of homosexual practice, as well as employees who express their religious faith within the walls of secular institutions. If such societies no longer execute dissidents, then that is largely because they can take for granted a far greater degree of social peace, thanks to unprecedented wealth, health, and political control. To be fair, it is also because Western societies have learned through gradual liberalization that social cohesion can survive a greater measure of plurality than was previously supposed. We should observe, however, that the issues of social cohesion and national identity in the face of cultural and moral diversity are still very much with us; and while traditionally the preoccupation of conservatives, they now disturb the sleep of post-multiculturalist liberals.

Second, insofar as Christendom was unjustly repressive, that can only be confessed and repudiated. Does such failure undermine Christianity's claim to a certain liberal humanism? Not necessarily. No human institution of longstanding can display a historical record that entirely consists with its anthropological and moral principles. Sin infects institutions—including churches—as well as individuals. Moreover, the fact that an institution from time to time betrays the principles that it daily affirms in its liturgy merely makes it inconsistent. It does not nullify its affirmation. Indeed, the institution deserves some credit for continuing to affirm the very principles by which its own conduct stands condemned. Inconsistency in virtue is surely better than consistency in vice.

So, third, insofar as Anglican ownership of slaves involved a denial of their equal humanity, then such self-betrayal can only be lamented unreservedly. However, it was never the Church as a whole that owned them, but rather one of its missionary bodies, the Society for the Propagation of the Gospel (S.P.G.).[18] It is true that the Archbishop of Canterbury was the Society's President;[19] but then two leading British abolitionists, Granville Sharp and William Wilberforce, were also members.[20] Further, in the judgement of one authority, the "blacks [on the S.P.G.'s Codrington planta-

18. I thank Diarmaid Macculloch for pointing this out to me—and also for his comments on the history of the Church of England in the sixteenth and seventeenth centuries, which have shaped what I have written in the paragraphs that follow. The responsibility for what appears there, of course, remains entirely mine.

19. Bennett, *Bondsmen and Bishops*, 124.

20. Jakobsson, *Am I Not a Man and a Brother?* 62, 254.

tion] were treated with unusual humanity."[21] More generally, Roger Anstey, the leading historian of British abolition, ascribes to Anglican (latitudinarian) theology an important role in "producing a cast of mind prepared to contemplate reform," by propagating the ideas of benevolence and of progressive revelation.[22] In the campaign for the abolition of the slave trade Anglican clergy comprised the largest group of supporters after the Quakers.[23] Moreover, according to Anstey, "[t]he record of the [Anglican] episcopal bench [in the House of Lords] ... was in fact good":[24] "the bench of bishops voted virtually en bloc for abolition when the motion came on [23 March 1807]."[25]

Fourth, the Anglican establishment did not penalize Roman Catholics or nonconformists because it doubted their equal humanity, but because it feared their political subversiveness. Likewise, it has not discriminated against women or gays because it doubted their equal status before God. In the case of women it has doubted that equality before God implies social equality or, more fastidiously, fitness for the role of priest or bishop; and in the case of gays it has doubted the morality of homosexual practice. Even liberal establishments countenance discrimination against classes of people on the grounds of their ill-suitedness to roles or their immoral behaviour, without calling into question their equal humanity.

Finally, the Church of England was originally conceived as a relatively liberal space, and, despite parts of itself, it has maintained a continuous liberal strand ever since. Determined to avoid importing continental-style civil bloodshed, Queen Elizabeth I settled the church as broadly Protestant. She refused Puritan pressure to make it strictly Calvinist, and she reluctantly ceded the active repression of English Roman Catholics only in the wake of military rebellion in 1569–70, and when it became clear that some

---

21. Bennett, *Bondsmen and Bishops*, 113.

22. Anstey, *The Atlantic Slave Trade and British Abolition, 1760–1810*, 126 and chapter 5 *passim*. Shortly after his death, David Brion Davis, himself a leading historian of American slavery, wrote of Anstey that "[n]o other historian on either side of the Atlantic has acquired a comparable mastery of ... the politics of British abolition and emancipation" ("An Appreciation of Roger Anstey," 11). Over three decades later Anstey's authority remains strong: in 2006 John Coffey wrote of *The Atlantic Slave Trade* that "this remains the finest academic account of British abolition" ("The Abolition of the Slave Trade," 9).

23. Anstey, *The Atlantic Slave Trade*, 261–62.

24. Ibid., 393 n.10.

25. Ibid., 393.

were reading the Pope's dissolution of her subjects' allegiance to her in 1570 as ground for plotting her assassination.

It is true, sadly, that in the following twelve decades the political persecution of Catholics and nonconformists was intermittently brutal. Nevertheless, even during that long period of sectarian hostility, civil war, and government repression, the Church of England managed to generate and sustain a liberal tradition. I refer immediately to the intellectual community that the convivial Lucius Carey, 2nd Viscount Falkland gathered around himself at his Oxfordshire home in the politically tense 1630s. Alarmed at the rising stridency of rival certainties and appalled by the ensuing violence, this "Great Tew Circle" championed the use of reason in matters of religion, followed Erasmus (and St. Paul) in distinguishing between *fundamenta* and *adiaphora*, advocated tolerance on matters indifferent, and looked for the reunion of Christendom.[26] The reasonable and pacific temper of this body of lay Anglicans is well expressed by Falkland himself in his discourse, *Of the Infallibility of the Church of Rome*":

> it is plaine, that he [the emperor Constantine] thought punishing for opinions to be a mark, which might serve to know false opinions by. . . . I am sure Christian Religions chiefest glory being, that it encreaseth by being persecuted; and . . . me thinks . . . everything is destroyed by the contrary to what settled and composed it. . . . I desire recrimination may not be used; for though it be true, that Calvin had done it, and the Church of England, a little (which is a little too much) . . . , yet she (confessing she may erre) is not so chargeable with any fault, as those which pretend they cannot, and so will be sure never to mend it; . . .
>
> I confess this opinion of damning so many, and this custome of burning so many, this breeding up those, who knew nothing else in any point of religion, yet to be in a readinesse to cry, *To the fire with him, to hell with him.* . . . These I say, in my opinion were chiefly the causes which made so many, so suddenly leave

---

26. The Great Tew Circle was accused of Socinian heterodoxy. In fact, they were Socinian only in the broad sense of advocating the use of reason in religion, not in the strict sense of being anti-Trinitarian (Trevor-Roper, *Catholics, Anglicans, and Puritans*, 188–89). As Falkland's close friend, Edward Hyde, Earl of Clarendon, wrote of him: he was Socinian only in "the having read Socinus, and the commending that in him, which nobody can reasonably discommend in him, and the making use of that reason that God has given a man for the examining of that which is most properly to be examined by reason, and to avoid the weak arguments of some men, . . . or to discover the fallacies of others." (*Animadversions upon a book, intituled, Fanaticism fanatically imputed to the Catholic Church*, 187–88).

the Church of Rome.... If any man vouchsafe to think, either this [discourse], or the authour of it, of value enough to confute the one, and informe the other, I shall desire him to do it ... with that temper, which is fit to be used by men that are not so passionate, as to have the definition of reasonable creatures in vaine, remembering that truth in likelyhood is, where her author God was, in the *still voice*, and not the *loud wind*.²⁷

And then, again, in Falkland's remarkably gracious response to a Roman Catholic critic:

> I am also to thank you ... for not mixing gall with your inke; since I have ever thought that there should bee as little bitterness in a treatise of controversie, as in a love-letter, and that the contrary way was void both of Christian charity, and humane wisedome, as serving onely ... to fright away the game, and make their adversarie unwilling to take instruction from him, from whom they have received injuries, and making themselves unabler to discover the truth (which Saint Au[gu]stine sayes is hard for him to find who is calme, but impossible for him that is angry).²⁸

The Great Tew Circle was not an ephemeral anomaly. It stood self-consciously in the tradition of Christian humanism, among whose patriarchs it counted Richard Hooker,²⁹ who argued in his classic apology for the Elizabethan settlement that "we must acknowledge even heretics themselves to be, though a maimed part, yet a part of the visible Church."³⁰ Yes, the Circle was scattered and, in part, consumed by the Civil War: Falkland himself was killed at the battle of Newbury and his more famous confrère, William Chillingworth, died as a prisoner-of-war. Nevertheless other members of the Circle survived, not least Gilbert Sheldon, who as Archbishop of Canterbury from 1663–77 helped to make the post-Restoration Anglican church "rational in method, ecumenical in its ultimate aims, ... conciliatory, not authoritarian."³¹ Moreover, Chillingworth's work, espe-

---

27. Carey, *Sir Lucius Cary, late Lord Viscount of Falkland*, 14–15, 25.

28. Carey, *The Lord of Faulkland's Reply*, in ibid., 51–52.

29. Griffin, *Latitudinarianism in the Seventeenth Century Church of England*, 89: "The characteristic thought of his [Falkland's] circle was consciously and directly in the tradition of sixteenth century Christian Humanism, with its stress on free will, theological minimalism, charity in inessentials, and a concern for morality above creedal speculation"; Trevor-Roper, *Catholics, Anglicans, and Puritans*, 189, 191, 194.

30. Hooker, *Of the Laws of Ecclesiastical Polity*, III.i.11, 347.

31. Trevor-Roper, *Catholics, Anglicans, and Puritans*, 218–19, 226, 228.

cially *The Religion of the Protestants* (1638), "saw a renaissance following the Restoration, . . . became dominant following the [Glorious] Revolution, . . . [and] marked an epochal shift in English theology from dogmatic system to a greater emphasis on the role of reason."[32] Over two hundred years after the Restoration, one eminent (Scottish) churchman judged that, while Falkland's moderate party was apparently swallowed up by the Civil War:

> the principles with which it was identified, and the succession of illustrious men who belong to it, made a far more powerful impression on the national mind than has been commonly supposed. The clear evidence of this is the virtual triumph of these principles, rather than those of either of the extreme parties [Puritan and Laudian], at the Revolution of 1688. . . . The same principles, both in Church and State, have never since ceased to influence our national thought and life. Their development constitutes one of the strongest, and—as it appears to me—one of the soundest and best strands, in the great thread of our national history.[33]

A few years later, the great Victorian critic, Matthew Arnold, chose to devote an essay to Falkland, writing of him as an early champion of the political liberty that was coming to prevail in his own time:

> Shall we blame him for his lucidity of mind and largeness of temper? Shall we even pity him? By no means. They are his great title to veneration. They are what make him ours; what link him with the nineteenth century. He and his friends, by their heroic and hopeless stand against the inadequate ideals dominant in their time, kept open their communications with the future, lived with the future. Their battle is ours too; and that we pursue it with fairer hopes of success than they did, we owe to their having waged it, and fallen.[34]

Let us pause here to take stock. Thus far, the story that I have told is as follows. A liberal humanist ethos and its supporting humanist anthropology

---

32. Pfizenmaier, *The Trinitarian Theology of Dr Samuel Clarke*, 43. Pfizenmaier cites Creighton, "Chillingworth, William." Creighton records that *The Religion of Protestants*, first published in two editions in 1638, was republished in 1664, 1674, 1684, 1687, and then—together with some other writings by Chillingworth—in 1704, 1719, 1722, 1727 and 1742.

33. Tulloch, *Rational Theology and Christian Philosophy in England in the 17th Century*, I.vi-vii. The most recent edition of the *Dictionary of National Biography* reckons this work "a still valuable analysis" (Bayne, "Tulloch, John").

34. Arnold, *Mixed Essays*, 232–33.

is a particular option, not a natural, default position. It is therefore subject to competition and vulnerable to being overwhelmed—as indeed it has been in living memory. Accordingly public institutions that would stay liberal need actively to promote a liberal ethos, and the humanist view of human being that makes sense of it. They also need to affirm larger worldviews that make sense of its humanist anthropology. There are various possibilities, not all of which can be affirmed simultaneously by the same institutions or in the same public rituals. One, therefore, needs to be chosen. In England, Anglican Christianity is—notwithstanding the blemishes on its historical record—the sitting, and not unworthy, candidate.

VI. Answering Two Objections to the Anglican Option

One obvious retort to this last part of my argument is that, while Anglicanism may be the sitting candidate, there is a better one standing. But is there? There are, of course, other, non-religious liberal humanisms. However, the extent to which these are intellectually viable apart from a theological basis is controversial; and it is controversial not only from the point of view of religious believers, but also in the eyes of some agnostic or atheist philosophers. Jürgen Habermas, for example, has admitted that religious traditions "have the distinction of a superior capacity for articulating our [liberal, humanist] moral sensibility";[35] and Raymond Gaita thinks that secular philosophical talk about inalienable human dignity and rights is just so much "whistling in the dark," such notions having no secure home outside of religious traditions.[36]

Nevertheless, it is conceivable that England could become sufficiently confident in some secular version of liberal humanism as to opt for its establishment instead of Anglican Christianity's. It could develop secularist public ceremonies to replace Christian ones—as has republican France. It could set about fostering liberal humanist virtues through secular equivalents of churches, liturgies, and Bible-study groups. This *could* happen, but there is little sign of a collective will to make it happen. What Edward Norman wrote in 2003 still seems true now: "There is no widely accepted theoretical or symbolical alternative to the Christian religion as the justification

---

35. Habermas, "Habermas entre démocratie et génétique," viii.
36. Gaita, *A Common Humanity*, 5.

of public moral consciousness."[37] There is no obvious challenger to the sitting candidate.

Another question that my argument obviously raises is this: Can the public privileging of a particular religion be compatible with the liberal right to religious freedom? Yes, it can; and in England it is. In the course of the eighteenth and nineteenth centuries, the penalties for religious nonconformity in England were gradually lifted, and non-Anglicans were permitted entry to universities, the armed services, and public office. The result now is that there is no public office in England that determines either law or public policy, which may not be filled with non-Anglicans, or non-Christians, or unbelievers.[38] Indeed, given a recent finding that 63 percent of Americans would be less likely to vote for a candidate who does not believe in God,[39] an agnostic or atheist today has a greater chance of becoming Prime Minister of the United Kingdom than President of the United States of America. Except on the point of a formal, institutional separation of church and state, contemporary England meets Nicholas Wolterstorff's criteria for a liberal democratic polity: namely, that "the state must not differentiate in its treatment of citizens on account of their religion or lack thereof, and there must be no differentiation among citizens in their right to voice in the conduct and personnel of the state on account of their religion or lack thereof."[40]

Prima facie evidence that the Anglican establishment is compatible with religious freedom is furnished by the support that many members of minority faiths give it. Indeed, Tariq Modood claimed in 1994 that it is "a brute fact" that not a single article or speech by any non-Christian faith in favour of disestablishment can be found;[41] and he wrote that "the minimal nature of the Anglican establishment, its proven openness to other denominations and faiths seeking public space, and the fact that its very existence is an ongoing acknowledgement of the public character of religion, are all reasons why it may be far less intimidating to the minority faiths than a triumphal secularism."[42]

37. Norman, *Secularisation*, 109.

38. The single remaining exception is that of the monarch, who may not be Roman Catholic. However, while the monarch remains the ultimate political authority in the British constitution, she neither formulates proposals for law or policy, nor does she determine whether such proposals are adopted.

39. Stiltner and Michels, "Religion, Rhetoric, and Running for Office," 261.

40. Wolterstorff, "Why Can't We All Just Get Along with Each Other?" 34.

41. Modood, "Establishment, Multiculturalism, and British Citizenship," 53.

42. Ibid., 72–73. Modood's statement now needs slight modification, since, according

The claim that the establishment of the Church of England is compatible with the exercise of religious freedom, receives *prima facie* corroboration from the support given it by adherents of minority faiths. According to Rex Ahdar, Professor of Law at the University of Otago, and Ian Leigh, Professor of Law at Durham University, it is also corroborated by international legal conventions and the case law of the European Convention on Human Rights.[43] U.S. First Amendment case law, which holds that the free exercise of religion can never be complete until Church and State are separated, is the global exception, not the rule.[44] At least two eminent American scholars of law, Michael Perry and John Witte, agree. Witte writes of the "conspicuous absen[ce]" in international legal norms of the more radical demands for separationism reified in the American metaphor of a wall of separation.[45]

Most U.S. commentators, however, regard the establishment of a particular religion as entailing a necessary offense against the equal dignity of nonconformists.[46] It implies a condescending tolerance, a "symbolic ostracism."[47] I do not find this point cogent. I can understand why public Christian theological affirmation might somewhat disturb non-Christian or non-theistic citizens. It might confront them with views with which they do not agree. It might contradict them. Yes, it might require them to tolerate a certain element of difference and foreignness in public institutions and rituals; but encounter with difference is a normal feature of social life, and tolerance is, after all, a classic liberal virtue. So why would it—*as such* and absent any restriction of civil or political liberties—offend their dignity as equal citizens?

As I see it, there can be no such thing as a public order that is morally, anthropologically, and metaphysically neutral. It must commit itself one way or another. In which case, it is inevitable that some members of any plural society will find themselves in a public order that affirms a worldview that is more or less different to their own; and will feel somewhat irritated

---

to Paul Weller (*Time for a Change*, 176), the (tiny) Buddhist community has come out against the Church of England's establishment.

43. Ahdar and Leigh, "Is Establishment Consistent with Religious Freedom?" 127.

44. Ibid., 154.

45. Ibid., 134.

46. For a rare American argument in favour of the "partial" or "constitutionally limited" establishment of religion, see Walker, "Illusory Pluralism, Inexorable Establishment."

47. So Steven Smith in Ahdar and Leigh, *Religious Freedom in the Liberal State*, 130.

by it. Secularist public institutions that refuse to make any theological affirmation need not be intentionally atheist; yet they are still not neutral. They cannot avoid implying that theological affirmation is unimportant for social health.[48] Many theistic citizens—not least Muslims—will disagree strongly with this implication, and feel somewhat disturbed by the studiously agnostic silence of public space. This alone, however, does not give them sufficient reason to feel that their dignity as equal citizens is being affronted. Not all contradiction amounts to objective offense.

But what about the fact that one worldview is privileged with establishment, and that others are therefore not quite equal? Well, unequal treatment need not imply lack of due respect. As Ahdar and Leigh argue, an historic religion that is supported more or less actively by a majority of citizens, and that performs valuable social, educational, and cultural functions, might deserve certain privileges.[49] Unequal treatment may have cogent reasons that do not amount to an offense against the equal human dignity of citizens. Inequality can still be equitable.[50]

---

48. Along very similar lines Graham Walker argues that American judges who rule that prayers in school are improper because of the impressionability of children "are strangely oblivious to the reverse implication of impressionability," namely, that children "are deeply susceptible to the politically sanctioned absence of God" and that banning school prayers disposes them to regard religion as only privately "true" ("Illusory Pluralism, Inexorable Establishment," 112). "Whatever the mechanism," he writes, "the effect is that of a religious establishment: the state promotes a preferred religious message, whether of indifference, equivalence, or incommensurability" (ibid., 114).

49. Ahdar and Leigh, *Religious Freedom in the Liberal State*, 146. Ahdar and Leigh's view here resonates with Charles Taylor's "communitarian liberalism," which affirms fundamental human liberties but allows other rights to be qualified by a public commitment to a certain vision of the good life: "[In the eyes of Quebeckers] a society can be organized around a definition of the good life, without this being seen as a depreciation of those who do not personally share this definition. . . . According to this conception, a liberal society singles itself out as such by the way in which it treats minorities, including those who do not share public definitions of the good, and above all by the rights it accords to all of its members. . . . [T]hey distinguish these fundamental rights from the broad range of immunities and presumptions of uniform treatment that have sprung up in modern cultures of judicial review. They are willing to weigh the importance of certain forms of uniform treatment against the importance of cultural survival. . . . I would endorse this model" (Taylor, "The Politics of Recognition," 59, 61).

50. I have borrowed this illuminating distinction from Paul Weller: "Arguably, in a society with a Christian inheritance and in which a comparatively large proportion of the population continues to identify in some way as Christian, a contextual and balanced understanding of 'equity' is needed more than a formal 'equality'" (*Time for a Change*, 175).

Although she is a proudly American opponent of religious establishment, Martha Nussbaum inadvertently corroborates this argument. On the one hand, she holds that, in affirming a particular religion as orthodox, a state necessarily reduces dissenters to second-class citizens, denying their basic equality[51] and sanctioning "dignitary affronts in the symbolic realm."[52] "Our [American] 'fixed star,'" she tells us, "is that no . . . [religious] orthodoxies are admissible."[53] Her solution is essentially Rawlsian:[54] "The hope is that public institutions can be founded on principles that all can share, no matter what their religion. Of course these institutions will have an ethical content, prominently including the idea of equal respect itself. But they should not have a religious content."[55] This amounts to Rawls's "overlapping consensus," comprising a set of "free-standing" moral principles endorsed by a variety of comprehensive doctrines.[56]

That is on the one hand. On the other hand, and without any visible embarrassment, Nussbaum admits that respect for individual conscience does *not* mean that every religion and worldview must be equally respected by government.[57] "Extreme views," which contradict or threaten the very foundations of the liberal constitutional order and the equality of citizens within it, must be resisted—certainly, if they seek to find practical embodiment, but even if their mere verbal expression becomes a threat. Such views "will not . . . be able to present their ideas in the political sphere on an equal basis with other ideas."[58] Nevertheless Nussbaum herself believes that in such a situation "*people* [as distinct from their menacing deeds and words] are all respected as equals."[59]

What Nussbaum fails to notice is that her preferred liberal polity would itself establish a public orthodoxy, from which dissenters—be they sexists or racists or xenophobes or simply religious believers who hold that

---

51. Nussbaum, *Liberty of Conscience*, 5, 67.

52. Ibid., 21.

53. Ibid., 18.

54. While she takes her bearings primarily from Roger Williams, the seventeenth-century founder of the colony of Rhode Island, Nussbaum finds that Williams' position is well represented by Rawls (ibid., 57–58).

55. Ibid., 23.

56. Ibid., 64–65, 68, 361.

57. Ibid., 24.

58. Ibid.

59. Ibid.

the public acknowledgement of God is basic to political health—will feel alienated. Some of them might even feel that their dignity is being affronted. According to Nussbaum, however, they need not. Ironically, therefore, she confirms that an established public orthodoxy of some sort is actually inevitable; that some are bound to find themselves more or less on the wrong side of it; and that contradiction, even suppression, of dissent need not amount to an offense against equal dignity.

VII. Popular Support for the Anglican Establishment

The justification for endowing the Church of England with the privilege of establishment, which I have so far advanced, is three-fold: first, that it represents a worldview that is supportive of a liberal humanist ethos; second, that its particular form of establishment has not involved civil and political penalties for non-Anglicans for well over a century;[60] and third, that its public orthodoxy can contradict the worldviews of some citizens without offending against their equal dignity. A fourth ground, which I add now, is that the Anglican establishment is supported more or less actively by a majority of citizens. I add this simply because it would be politically difficult (although neither impossible nor irrational) to maintain establishment in the face of an actively hostile democratic majority.[61]

But *is* the Church of England in fact supported by a majority of English citizens? Surely Britain is a secular country? Indeed, surely Britain is one of the most secular European countries, since so few of its population attend places of worship? A Tearfund survey of 7,000 adults throughout the United Kingdom in 2006 revealed that only 15 percent attend a Christian church *of any kind* at least once a month, with a further 10 percent attending somewhere between once a month and once a year.[62] Churchgoing is

---

60. Cranmer at al., *Church and State*, 41.

61. Maintaining establishment in the face of a hostile democratic majority need not be impossible: after all, elected Members of Parliament have been ignoring the popular majority in favour of capital punishment for decades. Nor need it be rationally indefensible, since popular majorities have been known to get it seriously wrong—as when 44 percent of the active German electorate voted the National Socialists into federal government in 1933.

62. Ashworth and Farthing, *Churchgoing in the UK*, 6. These figures are very similar to those recorded by the British Social Attitudes Survey of 2004 (ibid., 41). It is true that, between February 2006 and September 2007, the Tearfund figures for both monthly and annual attendance declined to 13 percent and 21 percent respectively; but it is also

therefore the sport of a minority—sizeable, perhaps, but still a clear minority. And Church-of-England-going is the sport of an even smaller minority.

On the other hand, 53 percent of those polled claimed affiliation with Christianity[63] and there is reason to suppose that such claims express more than a merely nominal association. The U.K. Government's Census of April 2001 returned 71.6 percent identifying themselves as Christian, which is a substantially larger proportion than that recorded by Tearfund. Why the discrepancy? The Tearfund report offers the following explanation. The Census' question was "What is your religion?" whereas Tearfund's question was "Do you regard yourself as belonging to any particular religion?" Affirmative answers to the former included some from people who would have baulked at confessing that they "belonged" to a religion, and whose affirmation was therefore simply nominal. What this implies is that affirmative answers to Tearfund's question were expressive of a more substantial commitment.[64]

More recently, 50 percent of respondents to the British Social Attitudes survey of 2008 identified themselves as "belonging" to the Christian religion; and 67 percent of respondents were classified as either "religious" (i.e., identifying with a religion, believing in God, and attending religious services) or "fuzzy faithful" (i.e., doing two out of those three).[65]

Moreover, there are empirical grounds for not assuming that non-churchgoers are completely lacking in sympathy for religious beliefs and practice. Of those Britons who reported to the 2001 Opinion Business Research poll that they did not go to church, 41 percent nevertheless admitted to praying.[66] Further still, of the one third of respondents classified

---

true that between September 2007 and September 2008 they climbed again by 2 percent and 5 percent (www.tearfund.org/News/Press+releases/Church+is+where+the+heart+is.htm, accessed on 2 May 2009).

63. Ashworth and Farthing, *Churchgoing in the UK*, 4.

64. Ibid.

65. Park et al., eds., *British Social Attitudes: The 26th Report*, 67 (Table 4.1) and 71 (Table 4.6). The Report on the 2008 British Social Attitudes survey contains a slight discrepancy. According to Table 4.6, 26 percent are "religious" (i.e., identify with a religion, believe in God, and attend services), 36 percent are "fuzzy faithful" (i.e., do two out of the three things that characterise the "religious"), and 31 percent are "unreligious" (i.e., do none of them). Later, however, these figures become 28 percent "religious," 39 percent "fuzzy faithful," and 33 percent "unreligious" (ibid., 90). This is probably due to the removal of non-respondents in the summary on page 90.

66. Ashworth and Farthing, *Churchgoing in the UK*, 1, citing the Opinion Business Research national poll of 2001.

as "unreligious" by the 2008 B.S.A. survey, 49 percent agreed that religion is beneficial in helping people find inner peace or happiness, 42 percent scored 3 to 4 on a fourteen point scale of religiosity, and only 3 percent scored 0.[67]

It seems to me, therefore, that it cannot be presumed that a democratic majority of British people is currently impervious or hostile to religious beliefs, symbols, and practices, and unappreciative of their public affirmation; and since Christianity is the religion with which the vast majority of Britons is familiar, it cannot be presumed that a democratic majority is completely alienated from it.

It is true, as R. M. Morris has argued,[68] that, if current trends continue, remaining sympathy for religion will probably diminish. Yet since current trends run more on indifference than anticlericalism (as Morris himself notes), there is reason to hope that they could be reversed by alerting people to the fragility of liberal humanist culture and to the importance of the Christian church to its prosperity. A commitment to humanity is one good reason for believing in God.

British people who identify themselves as Christian or who are sympathetically disposed, of course, might still object to the public, institutional affirmation of any religion. There is evidence, however, that they do not object. In a B.B.C. poll in February 2009 almost two-thirds (63 percent) of those questioned—and more or less equally across age-groups—said that the law "should respect and be influenced by U.K. religious values." A similar proportion (62 percent) agreed that "religion has an important role to play in public life," although here support was actually higher among the young than among the middle-aged and elderly.[69] Moreover, 79 percent of Muslims polled, and almost as many Hindus (74 percent) and Sikhs (74 percent), affirmed the shaping of law by "U.K. religious values."[70]

Now, support for the shaping of law by "U.K. religious values" does not quite add up to support for the establishment of Anglican Christianity. However, given that most of those describing themselves as Christian would tick the "Church of England" box, and given what we know about

---

67. Park, *British Social Attitudes*, 72 (Table 4.7) and 92 (Figure 5.1).

68. Morris, *Church and State in 21st Century Britain*, 169–71.

69. In response to the question, "Do you agree with the statement that religion has an important role to play in public life?" affirmative answers were given by 77 percent of 18–24 year olds and 65 percent of 25–34 year olds (http://news.bbc.co.uk/1/hi/uk/7783563.stm and http://news.bbc.co.uk/1/hi/uk/7906595.stm, accessed on 2 May 2009).

70. Ibid.

the predominantly supportive views of minority faith communities, of Roman Catholics,[71] and of Protestant nonconformists,[72] it is reasonable to infer support for the Anglican establishment.

VIII. Conclusion

Every nation has an understanding of the nature and forms of human flourishing, and in each case this understanding will include elements of peculiar insight. All other things being equal, therefore, each nation should have the freedom—the autonomy—to incarnate this understanding and insight in its own way of life, and to develop it in its own terms. This is because its terms might prove better and wiser than others, in which case other nations will benefit by learning them.

Insofar as its customs and institutions embody human goods, a nation has a duty to defend them. Part of this defence will consist of policing its borders, so as to moderate immigration and preserve the cultural

---

71. My claim about the view of the Anglican establishment that prevails among Roman Catholics is perforce less than scientific. Nevertheless, in support I can cite three eminent English Roman Catholics. In an article in the *Times* newspaper on 30 March 2009 William Rees-Mogg stated that "[f]ew Catholics want to see the Church of England disestablished" ("Reform the Monarchy? Let's Wait for a Century"). In his 2008 book, *The Realm: An Unfashionable Essay on the Conversion of England*, Aidan Nicholls, O.P., wrote that "[o]ne does not have to be Anglican to be worried by the thought of disestablishment," before proceeding to quote Edward Norman in its support (78). And in his 1997 essay, "The Case for Retaining the Establishment," the Roman Catholic historian Adrian Hastings reckoned that "a weak establishment may well be the best basis for the maintenance of a constructive dualism.... [I]t remains in principle right, even wonderful, that ... [the presence of Anglican bishops in the House of Lords should] be part of our constitution" (in Modood, *Church, State, and Religious Minorities*, 41–42, 46).

72. R. M. Morris concedes only that contemporary nonconformists in England oppose the principle of establishment "without the stridency or vehemence of old" (*Church and State in 21st Century Britain*). This, however, seems to be rather less than the whole truth. Paul Weller (*Time for a Change*, 169, 184), at once social scientist and Baptist minister, observes that since the late nineteenth century the Free Churches have gradually moved away from calling for the abolition of the establishment to pressing for accommodation within it, seeing it as a bulwark against ideological secularism. The Methodist Church's 2004 *Report on Church, State, and Establishment* confirms Weller's reading. It observes that there is no single view of establishment among contemporary Methodists; and it does not observe that support for disestablishment predominates. Instead, it entertains a range of possible relationships between church and state, which may be theologically valid according to the circumstances (ss.108, 111.v). These include an Anglican establishment that involves non-Anglican Christians in genuinely open ways that do not patronize (ss.113, 115, 116, 117).

consensus necessary to keep its customs and institutions intelligible and morally authoritative. But another part will consist of the public affirmation of views that support its characteristic embodiment of human goods. Not all views will support it; some will undermine it. An unconstrained libertarian, multiculturalist free-for-all is, therefore, not a responsible option. Even the great modern liberal patriarch, John Rawls, recognized that—as does his disciple, Martha Nussbaum. They do not dispute the need for a public orthodoxy of some kind.

Dispute arises over its content. For Rawls, the public orthodoxy should comprise liberal values and virtues, which he claims can be made to "float free" of the larger "comprehensive doctrines" or worldviews that support them. I doubt this—as do a number of philosophers, some eminent, some atheist, and some both. Rawls admits that a liberal ethos is vulnerable to the ascendancy of "unreasonable comprehensive doctrines," but only implies the consequent need to suppress those doctrines. Once this implication is made explicit, it becomes clear that his public orthodoxy includes not only a liberal ethos, but also (at least indirectly) the defence of supportive doctrines against hostile ones.

Rawls is correct to believe that a liberal ethos can find support in a range of different worldviews—views that I classify as humanist. But if that is the case, how can a single nation-state publicly affirm multiple humanist doctrines in its institutions and public rituals? One way is for it to adopt as its public creed a vague, monotheistic deism, under which umbrella at least the several religious humanisms can huddle more or less comfortably. This, arguably, is what the United States has done—and given its historical origins partly in a reaction against highly coercive forms of religious establishment, it could have done no other. In England, however, history has taken a different course. The English state's establishment of Anglican Christianity has survived, but become increasingly less coercive and more generous. Now most non-Anglican Christians, most non-Christian religious believers, and even many who practice no religion at all support the Anglican establishment-lite, because they recognize the benefits it brings to the whole national community. The English arrangement, therefore, offers another model of public orthodoxy—one where the state affirms a single humanist comprehensive doctrine, but where the manner of its affirmation is sufficiently generous and hospitable as to allow other kinds of humanist to identify with it, if not to own it fully.

3

Sovereignty and Responsibility

I. Responsibility within and beyond Sovereignty

National autonomy is a good, of which nations should have a measure. It is a good because it gives a nation the freedom to incarnate universal human goods in creative ways that correspond to its distinctive circumstances and historical experiences. Thus different nations bear witness to the created moral order in different ways, ordering human goods in different hierarchies and discerning different practical implications. Some nations achieve a better grasp than others. Each offers the others their own peculiar moral wisdom. As each human individual is responsible under God to incarnate, defend, and promote created goods, so are bodies of individuals, including nations.

This concept of national autonomy differs significantly from the notion of national sovereignty that has dominated contemporary international law until very recently. According to a strictly textual reading of the law, each nation has a right to defend itself unilaterally against foreign attack, except where an attack is authorized by the United Nations' Security Council to stop the likes of genocide. What this implies is that, unless the Security Council decides to acknowledge very grave and massive injustice, and to authorize military action against it, nation-states are free, in the eyes of the law, to do as they please within their borders. They are legally sovereign and their conduct is immune from interference.[1] In contrast, the kind of

---

1. Since 2005 the legal picture has become more complicated. At its World Summit

national autonomy that I have defended is only the moral right to incarnate and explicate human goods in distinctive ways—the right to exercise responsibility toward the universal moral order in a creative fashion—and not an immunity against responsibility altogether.

This Christian concept of morally responsible autonomy takes its cue from Hugo Grotius, not from Thomas Hobbes. According to Hobbes, the human condition is at base a state of nature, where each is at war with all and there is only one natural law or right—that of self-preservation. Only when individuals—or, by extension, nation-states—opt into a social agreement or contract or treaty do other rights and obligations come into being. In other words, only when there is civil or positive law does right or justice amount to anything more than self-preservation—and even then, self-preservation will lie at its root. In contrast, Grotius' view is more Thomist, more Christian, and more biblical. He denies that nature inclines human beings simply to seek their own private advantage, and that the law is simply instituted for the sake of interest.[2] "Man is indeed an animal," he writes, "but one of a very high order, and that excels all the other species of animals much more than they differ from one another. . . . Now amongst things peculiar to man, is his desire of society";[3] and "[t]his sociability . . . or this care of maintaining society . . . is the fountain of right, properly so called."[4] Accordingly, while the animal instinct for self-preservation finds "nothing repugnant to war,"[5] "right reason, and the nature of society" prohibit violence that is "repugnant

---

that year the United Nations endorsed the doctrine of the Responsibility to Protect (R2P), first propounded by the Canadian government's International Commission on Intervention and State Sovereignty in 2001, in that it affirmed that every state has the responsibility to protect its population from genocide, war crimes, ethnic cleansing, and crimes against humanity. This amounted to world-wide recognition, for the first time, of a state's *moral* responsibility within its own borders. Nevertheless, the U.N. confirmed that a state failing in its moral responsibility would still be immune from military interference—would still be legally sovereign—should the Security Council be unable, through political disagreement, to authorise action.

2. Grotius, *The Rights of War and Peace*, "The Preliminary Discourse," VI, 79.

3. Ibid.

4. Ibid., 85–86. Grotius does not deny that profit or advantage is "annexed" to the law of nature, "to the end that we might more eagerly affect society" (XVII, 93–94). Nevertheless, he holds that "human nature itself, which, though even the necessity of our circumstances should not require it, would of itself create in us a mutual desire of society (XVII, 93). The "most judicious philosophers" are correct, he tells us, to claim that friendship is not only founded on indigence, "for it is evident we are prompted to it by natural inclination" (II.I.IX.3, 405).

5. Ibid., I.II.3, 182–83.

Sovereignty and Responsibility

to society, that is, which invades another's right."⁶ In other words, there are *two* original principles, not just one: self-preservation *and* sociability. From this it follows that, where civil society with its positive law and courts and police are lacking, we are not left with a moral desert where no holds are barred in the pursuit of self-preservation. Writing of war between nation-states, Grotius says: "Let it be granted then, that laws must be silent in the midst of arms, provided they are only those laws that are civil and judicial, and proper for times of peace; but not those that are of perpetual obligation, and are equally suited to all times."⁷ Before international treaties and international law—and in their absence—stands natural right. Even where there is no law to enforce, there may still be injustice to punish: "right still subsists when the way to legal justice is not open," for example, where there is no (global) civil government;⁸ the power of punishing is not "properly an effect of civil jurisdiction," but "proceeds from the law of nature";⁹ and "it is not to be doubted, but that before the penal law be made, an offence may be punished."¹⁰ From this follows a natural right to intervene militarily for humanitarian purposes. Sovereigns, writes Grotius, "have a right to exact punishments, not only for injuries committed against themselves, or their subjects, but likewise, for those which do not peculiarly concern them, but which are, in any persons whatsoever, grievous violations of the law of nature or nations." Indeed, "it is so much more honourable, to revenge other peoples [*sic*] injuries rather than their own, by as much as it is more to be feared, lest out of a sense of their own sufferings, they either exceed the just measure of punishment, or, at least, prosecute their revenge with malice."¹¹ As an example of a grievous violation of the law of nature worthy of military contradiction Grotius cites cannibalism¹²—as had Francisco de Vitoria before him, together with human sacrifice.¹³

6. Ibid., I.II.3, 184.
7. Ibid., "The Preliminary Discourse," XXVII, 102.
8. Ibid., I.III.II, 241.
9. Ibid., II.XX.XL.4, 1024.
10. Ibid., II.XX.XXII.1, 996.
11. Ibid., II.XX.XL.1, 1021.
12. Ibid., II.XX.XL.3, 1022.
13. Vitoria, "On Dietary Laws, or Self-Restraint," I.5.5, 225. Vitoria, however, makes a point of saying that not *every* violation of the natural law deserves to be stopped by military means, only those that involve *iniuria* to others. Francisco Suárez agrees: military intervention can only be justified "in circumstances in which the slaughter of innocent people, and similar wrongs take place" ("On Charity: Disputation XIII," Section V.5, 826).

What this Grotian view asserts is that the rulers of nation-states are not sovereign in the sense that they have a moral right to do as they please within their own borders. Even where there is no social contract between nations, or where the international institutions established by contract fail to do adequate justice, there still remains natural right or justice; and among the obligations of natural justice is one that binds rulers not to grossly oppress their own peoples, and another that binds them to rescue foreign peoples from gross oppression. I said earlier that this Grotian view is Thomist, Christian, and biblical. How so? It is Thomist in its assertion that there is a *natural* moral law that applies universally and is prior to all human, positive law; and, more specifically, in its assertion that the natural law is rooted in a natural inclination to society as well as to self-preservation. This Thomist assertion of natural law is Christian, because it is biblical. That is, it affirms that the world is the creation of one God, that it therefore reflects its Creator's unity of mind and will, that it is ordered and not chaotic, and that this order is moral as well as physical. What the biblical, and therefore Christian, understanding of God and of the world in relation to him implies is that morality is a discovery before it is an invention. It is not invented *ab initio*, conjured out of nothing. Its principles are given in the created nature of things, and all human moral creativity is properly responsible—that is to say, a response to what has first been given.

The Thomist assertion that the principles of natural law comprise an attraction to the good of society, as well as to the good of self-preservation, is also Christian, because it is biblical. In the book of Genesis' first creation story, we are told seven times that, sitting back and contemplating his creation, "God saw that it was good."[14] Among the creatures that God created good are human beings; what is good deserves respect and care; human beings therefore deserve respect and care. It follows that each human being has a duty of respect and care both toward herself and toward her fellow humans. Accordingly, Jesus commands us to love our neighbors *as* we love ourselves.[15]

II. The Authority of International Law, and Its Limits

The Christian vision of national and international affairs is not Hobbesian. Before there are social contracts, and in their absence, there is natural

---

14. Gen 1:4, 10, 12, 18, 21, 25, 31.
15. Matt 22:30; Mark 12:31; Luke 10:27.

moral law. This serves to relativize the importance of international treaties and derivative law, but not to negate it. Christian thinkers in the sixteenth and seventeenth centuries were quite aware of the problem of entrusting international affairs to the consciences of the rulers of nation-states: namely, the opportunities for self-delusion, if not outright manipulation, where the judge of a case is himself an interested party. Thus Francisco Suárez writes:

> it cannot be denied that in this matter [of public vengeance], one and the same person assumes, in a sense, the role of plaintiff and that of judge.... But the cause... is simply that this act of punitive justice has been indispensable to mankind, and that no more fitting method for its performance could, in the order of nature and humanly speaking, be found.... Neither is this case analogous to that of a private individual. For... such an individual is guided by his own [unaided] judgement, and therefore he will easily exceed the limits of vengeance; whereas public authority is guided by public counsel, to which heed must be paid.[16]

Grotius writes similarly: while "it is much honester, and more conducive to the peace of mankind, that differences should be decided by a third person that is disinterested, than that every man should be allowed to do himself justice in his own cause, wherein the illusions of self-love are much to be apprehended,"[17] outside of civil government that option is not available.[18]

What this line of thinking says is that, ideally, injustice should be fended off and punished in a universal sovereign state, according to universal laws, and by universal courts and police (setting aside all anxieties about such a state's propensity to tyranny). In their absence, however, unilateral belligerency can be justified in response to proportionately grave injustice, whether unjust invasion by an aggressor or another sovereign's maltreatment of his own people. Not all justice takes place in courts; and some must take place without them. The international state of nature is not a moral wasteland, bereft of moral law or conscience; and conscientious rulers can exercise the virtues of fairness and temperance in judging and punishing unjust enemies.

Of course, the international context of de Vitoria, Suárez, and Grotius was significantly different from our own. They lived at a time when such

---

16. Suárez, "On Charity: Disputation XIII," IV.7, 819.
17. Grotius, *The Rights of War and Peace*, I.III.I, 241.
18. Ibid., I.III.II, 241.

supranational authority as medieval popes and Holy Roman Emperors had exercised was being repudiated by newly Protestant rulers. We, on the other hand, live in an international context where individual nation-states have subscribed to international treaties and are thus bound by international law to acknowledge the authority of supranational bodies such as the General Assembly and Security Council of the United Nations, and the International Court of Justice at the Hague. In our age the realm of international affairs is not bereft of law or courts or publicly authorized enforcement. This is important, because, insofar as international institutions succeed both in doing justice *and in showing the scrupulous fairness by which it is done*, they increase the likelihood that justice will be *felt* to be done and that the judgements that do it will be accepted. In this way, the institutionalization of justice helps to reduce the risk of resentment at adverse judgements, and so to augment the public peace.

Nevertheless, the making of laws, the public appointment of judges to interpret them, and the scrupulous observance of regular procedures in the course of adjudication do not guarantee that justice will result. The laws can be perverse, the judges corrupt, and the procedures susceptible of manipulation by the guilty. Sometimes the legal system ends up *protecting* criminals from justice. Thus Grotius, appealing to Seneca, distinguishes right from justice, defining right merely as that which is actionable in the courts.[19]

However, even where a legal system does shield criminals from justice, there is still a strong reason to obey the law. There are good moral reasons of a prudential sort why we should be loath to transgress positive law even for the noblest of motives. The case for this is made with memorable rhetorical force in *A Man for all Seasons*, Robert Bolt's play about Sir Thomas More. In one scene More is urged by his daughter, Margaret, and his future son-in-law, Nicholas Roper, to arrest Richard Rich, an informer. The subsequent argument rises to this climax:

> **Margaret (exasperated, pointing after Rich):** While you talk, he's gone!
>
> **More:** And go he should if he was the Devil himself until he broke the law!
>
> **Roper:** So now you'd give the Devil benefit of law!
>
> **More:** Yes. What would you do? Cut a great road through the law to get after the Devil?

---

19. Ibid., III.X.I.3, 1413–14.

Roper: I'd cut down every law in England to do that!

More: Oh? And when the last law was down, and the Devil turned round on you—where would you hide, Roper, the laws all being flat? This country's planted thick with laws from coast to coast—Man's laws, not God's—and if you cut them down—and you're just the man to do it—d'you really think you could stand upright in the winds that would blow then? Yes, I'd give the Devil benefit of law, for my own safety's sake.[20]

The effective social authority of law—that is, its power to order a society, whether national or international, and to safeguard the rights of its members—depends upon the willingness to obey of those whom it commands; and the willingness of each to obey depends partly on the law's being generally observed. It is reasonable for one party to obey the law so long as others generally do so too. It is reasonable for one to suffer the constraints of law, so long as others suffer them as well. If one party were to take the law into his own hands, even for motives that seem noble in his own eyes, then why shouldn't others do likewise? Well-intentioned vigilantism can pave the road to anarchy quite as much as malicious law-breaking; and in anarchy the strong are set entirely free to trample on the weak—*the laws all being flat*. So the virtue of prudence instructs us to give even the Devil benefit of law for our own safety's sake.

That is true. But the following is also true. Voluntary obedience will only be forthcoming so long as those who remain subject to the law are confident that those who break it will not retain the unfair advantages they have thereby seized—that is, so long as they are confident that the law will be enforced against law-breakers. If the law is not so enforced, and if law-breakers are seen to secure unfair advantage relative to the law-abiding, then the respect of the latter for the law will be shaken and its authority diminished. If this diminution proceeds far enough, then the rule of law will disintegrate and society will dissolve into anarchy. There are, then, *two* ways in which the law's authority can be undermined: first, by individuals—be they persons or states—taking the law into their own hands; and second, by the failure of public authorities to enforce the law against law-breakers. And sometimes, of course, the two are causally related. Sometimes, it is *because* public authorities have failed to enforce the law that individuals or states are moved to enforce it themselves.

This, for example, is exactly the scenario that Prime Minister Tony Blair strove to avoid in the months prior to April 2003, when the invasion

---

20. Bolt, *A Man for all Seasons*, 38–39.

of Iraq was finally launched. Mr. Blair's concern was not so much that Iraq was on the verge of posing an immediate threat to the United Kingdom through its possession of weapons of mass destruction (W.M.D.). Rather his concern was as follows: that Iraq was clearly intent on acquiring W.M.D.; that her possession of them would pose a grave and intractable threat to international peace; that the United Nations itself had recognized this by issuing seventeen Resolutions aimed at ensuring Iraq's disarmament; that Iraq had consistently striven to avoid bowing to the express will of the U.N. for over a decade; that only the repeated threat of military invasion had secured its reluctant and temporary compliance; and that, if the U.N. did not show itself willing to carry out that threat in the enforcement of its own resolutions, then the United States, made impatient by the experience of 9/11, would do so instead. Mr. Blair's concern was that the U.N.'s chronic failure to uphold international law would goad the U.S. into unilateral action. Here is Mr. Blair in his enormously impressive speech to the House of Commons on 18 March 2003:

> Of course Iraq is not the only part of this threat [i.e., of W.M.D. finding their way into the hands of terrorists]. But it is the test of whether we treat the threat seriously. Faced with it, the world should unite. The U.N. should be the focus, both of diplomacy and of action. That is what [Resolution] 1441 said. That was the deal. And I say to you, to break it now, to will the ends but not the means, that would do more damage in the long term to the U.N. than any other course.
>
> To fall back into the lassitude of the last twelve years, to talk, to discuss, to debate but never act; to declare our will but not enforce it; to combine strong language with weak intentions: a worse outcome than never speaking at all. And then, when the threat returns from Iraq or elsewhere, who will believe us? What price our credibility with the next tyrant? . . .
>
> I have come to the conclusion after much reluctance that the greater danger to the U.N. is inaction: that to pass Resolution 1441 and then refuse to enforce it would do the most deadly damage to the U.N.'s future strength, confirming it as an instrument of diplomacy but not of action, forcing nations down the very unilateralist path we wish to avoid.[21]

It is reasonable, it is in everyone's interests, it is in the interests of general peace that individuals and individual states should delegate the

---

21. Blair, "Full Statement to the House of Commons, 18 March 2003," 336–37.

enforcement of law and order to a body that will actually perform it. The problem with international law as it now stands, however, is that it denies the right of member states to use military force unilaterally except in self-defence, while reserving the enforcement of international law to a body (the Security Council) whose capacity to act is hamstrung by international politics and by the right of veto. By way of demonstrating why this is a problem, let me offer this analogy. A neighbor a few houses away is beating his own children to death. It is against the law for us to intervene directly, so we call the police and ask them to intervene instead. Before they can intervene, however, the police have to get authorization from a committee, any member of which can veto it. In this case a member of the committee is allied to the neighbor in some way. He therefore casts his veto and prevents the police from intervening. What are we to do? Shall we break the law and intervene unilaterally? Or shall we abide by the law and watch the children being done to death? That is the predicament into which current international law can deliver us. Individual nations are forbidden to intervene militarily in the affairs of another sovereign state, unless authorized by the Security Council of the U.N. to do so; but the power of the Security Council to issue authorization depends upon the political interests of its members. This was the case of Kosovo in 1999, when Russia made it clear that it would veto any intervention by N.A.T.O. to save the Kosovar Albanians from Serb troops, partly because of its cultural links with Serbia and partly because it did not want to set a precedent that might tie its hands in dealing with insurgents in Chechnya. As things now stand, the next time a Hitler decides to slaughter masses of his own people within the borders of his own state, is not dissuaded from this policy by diplomatic or economic pressure, and restrains himself from invading a neighbor; should this slaughter not qualify strictly as "genocide"; and should any member of the Security Council have an interest in vetoing the authorisation of intervention; then we would be required by law to stand by and watch. It therefore seems to me to be a grave problem with current international law that it *both* outlaws unauthorized intervention to stop mass atrocities or to topple a regime widely acknowledged to be grossly and chronically atrocious, *and* may refuse to give authorization.

III. The Possibility of Moral Illegality

Given this situation, there could be sufficiently strong *moral* reasons for breaking international law under certain conditions. While the authority of human positive and customary law is important and not to be brushed aside lightly, the authority of natural moral law is prior and superior; and where human law is absent or perverse *or fails*, natural moral law still obtains. Thus Grotius asserts, not only that "the antient liberty [of avenging injustice], which the law of nature at first gave us, remains still in force where there are no courts of justice," but that it also obtains "when complaint having been made to the judge, he does not render justice in a certain time."[22] If natural moral law does not sometimes trump human law, then, for example, those German citizens who plotted to kill Hitler in the assassination attempt of July 1944 were simply criminal traitors and not also, and foremost, moral heroes. Once it is recognized that there is a natural moral authority higher than that of positive law, then it follows that, while in some cases morality obliges us to obey the law even when wicked people appear to be getting away with murder, lest in the rash pursuit of justice we knock all the laws flat; in other cases it permits or obliges us to break the law in order to rescue victims from wicked people, lest in our chronic failure to do justice we expose all positive laws to contempt.

IV. The Marks of Morally Justified Military Intervention

Immediately, of course, this idea raises the urgent question of how we are to distinguish the cases. How can we tell unauthorized intervention that is justified from that which is not?[23] First, given the terrible destructiveness and hazardous unpredictability of even justified military intervention, the reason for embarking upon it has to be proportionately grave. The only kind of proportionately grave reason that international law specifies is genocide—and that, arguably, is still intended only as a motive for military intervention that is authorized by the Security Council. Morally speaking, however, it is arguable that murderous oppression on a massive scale that

---

22. Grotius, *The Rights of War and Peace*, II.XX.VIII.5, 970.

23. I take it that what I mean here by "morally justified" is what most discussion of these matters means by "legitimate" (as distinct from "legal"). For reasons best known to itself contemporary discourse prefers to refer to moral considerations obliquely. See, for example, Gareth Evans in *The Responsibility to Protect*, ch. 6.

is not strictly genocidal could be grave enough to warrant risking the evils and hazards of war. It seems to me, for example, that saving Kosovar Albanians from indiscriminate killing by the troops of a Serbian regime that had Srebrenica on its curriculum vitae was proportionate cause. Therefore, I agree with the report of the International Commission on Intervention and State Sovereignty, *The Responsibility to Protect*,[24] that just cause should be extended beyond genocide to include any "large scale loss of life" or "large scale 'ethnic cleansing.'"[25]

However, must the atrocity be "actual or [imminently] apprehended [that is, anticipated]" for intervention to be warranted—as the report stipulates?[26] One obvious reason for such a condition is that only then could intervention claim to be about protecting victims. After the event is over, there is presumably no protecting left to do. Well, actually, no. A regime that has shown itself willing to carry out mass atrocities, and which succeeds in doing so with impunity, will have no compunction about perpetrating fresh atrocities, should it see fit to do so. For that reason the international community has a responsibility to punish state atrocities after the fact, and not merely to stop them in mid-flight. *The Responsibility to Protect* comes close to my point here when it says that while "[o]verthrow of regimes is not, as such, a legitimate objective," "disabling that regime's capacity to harm its own people may be essential to discharging the mandate of protection—and what is necessary to achieve that disabling will vary from case to case. Occupation of territory may not be able to be avoided . . ."[27] In the light of this qualification, it seems to me that a case could be made for the invasion of Iraq in 2003 in terms of the need to keep weapons of mass destruction out of the hands of a regime that had been responsible for the murder of approximately 400,000 of its own citizens in the previous fifteen years, and which had already shown itself ready to use such weapons in its mass murdering on more than one occasion.

Other marks or criteria of morally justified but legally unauthorized military intervention, which *The Responsibility to Protect* lays down, are the usual just-war-doctrine-suspects: namely, that the intention must be

24. The International Commission on Intervention and State Sovereignty's report, *The Responsibility to Protect*, stipulates that for military intervention to be warranted, "there must be serious and irreparable harm *occurring to human beings, or imminently likely to occur*" (32 [s.4.18]. My emphasis).

25. Ibid., 32–33 (s.4.19–21).

26. Ibid., 32 (s.4.18–19).

27. Ibid., 35 (s.4.33).

to halt or avert (unjust) human suffering; that it should be a last resort, every other *available* and *effective* alternative having been tried; that the military means (and their destructiveness) should be proportionate—that is, limited to what is necessary to protect (and so punish); and that there must be a reasonable prospect of success—success being taken to include *both* military victory *and* postwar reconstruction.[28]

In addition to these necessary criteria of moral justification, there are two others that serve at least to mitigate the lack of legal authorization.[29] One is the intention to enforce international law in the form of the express will of the U.N. In other words, while breaking international law in its chosen *means*, unauthorized intervention would nevertheless maintain respect for the law in its chosen *ends*. Judging by Tony Blair's account of its rationale in his House of Commons' speech, the invasion of Iraq in 2003 bore this mark.

The case of Kosovo highlights a second mitigating mark: that military intervention, though unauthorized by the Security Council, should nevertheless be undertaken by a broad alliance of states. The significance of this is that the broader the alliance, the less likely it is that the motives for intervention are purely private, rapaciously self-interested ones. With regard to Kosovo, some ideologically blinkered critics of N.A.T.O.'s intervention—such as Harold Pinter—were determined to view it as yet another instance of U.S. imperialism. "The truth is," wrote Pinter, "that neither Clinton nor Blair gives a damn about the Kosovar Albanians. This action has been yet another blatant and brutal assertion of U.S. power using N.A.T.O. as its missile. It sets out to consolidate one thing—American domination of Europe."[30] But N.A.T.O. was not just composed of the U.S.A. It was a body of nineteen nations, whose history did not display a uniform record of deference to its senior, American, member. Earlier in the 1990s European nations had proven perfectly capable of distancing themselves from U.S. foreign policy when they saw fit to do so—for example, over Iraq. Further,

---

28. Ibid., 35–37 (ss.4.32–43).

29. One way to square the circle between the competing claims of legality and moral legitimacy is by way of the courtroom process of a "plea in mitigation." Accordingly, a state would admit that it is violating international law by intervening without the Security Council's authorization, thereby acknowledging the law's authority; but it would then proceed to make a case for its transgression in terms of exceptional and defensible circumstances. This has been proposed by, among others, Thomas Franck and Michael Byers & Simon Chesterman (Evans, *The Responsibility to Protect*, 147).

30. As reported in *The Guardian*, 7 June 1999.

Sovereignty and Responsibility

in the forefront of N.A.T.O.'s military intervention stood France, which had made a post-war career out of not doing whatever the U.S. wants. Further still, America's own military involvement in Kosovo was patently reluctant—to the frustration of at least one European leader, Tony Blair; and this American reluctance was readily intelligible in the light of the fact that its national interest in the outcome of this Balkan conflict, as distinct from the interest of its European allies, was so slight. Even further, while it is true that one of N.A.T.O.'s member-states, Turkey, did have ties of ethnic and cultural kinship to the victims of the crime, it was the only one; and this interest was balanced by the ties of another member-state, Greece, to their oppressor. The size and the diversity of N.A.T.O., then, was *prima facie* evidence that its intervention in Kosovo was not motivated not by selfish national interests.

V. The Morality of "Hypocritical" Intervention

One of the most common ways of objecting to humanitarian justifications of unauthorized military intervention is to cast doubt on its sincerity by pointing to inconsistency of practice. The argument runs thus:

> You say that you care about the victims of oppression in country A. If that is *really* so, why didn't you intervene to save the victims in countries B, C, and D? The fact that you didn't intervene in those cases shows that you don't really care; and it implies that your claims to care in this case are hypocritical. Your real reason for intervening in A must therefore be something else, some selfish material or geopolitical interest.

Accordingly, the fact that the U.S. and other Western countries did not intervene in Rwanda or Kurdish Turkey or the Krajina (where 600,000 Serbs were "ethnically cleansed" by the Croats in 1995) is taken to imply that N.A.T.O.'s intervention in Kosovo was not genuinely humanitarian. And the fact that the West did not intervene in Chechnya or Tibet is taken as evidence that its intervention in Iraq or Afghanistan must have been selfish.

There are two ways of responding to the charge of hypocritical inconsistency. One is to say that even if we should have intervened in other places, that would still not amount to a reason not to have intervened here—unless there were some virtue in maintaining, as one journalist very nicely put it, "a level apathy field."[31] Surely, it is better to be inconsistently responsible than consistently irresponsible.

Another response to the charge is to deny it altogether and to say, "There were good moral reasons why we *didn't* intervene in B, C, and D; and there were good moral reasons why we *did* intervene in A." These moral reasons can be of three kinds: practical, prudential, or political. One reason why the U.S. and others intervened in Kosovo was that there was to hand an international body that had the political cohesion and military power to act effectively—namely, N.A.T.O. This was not the case in Rwanda. So one reason why Western countries did not intervene there was *practical:* effective means were not readily available to them. But how is a practical reason also a moral one? In this sense: that, except *in extremis*, one ought not to attempt even a worthy goal by means that are likely to fail.

A second moral reason that justifies intervention in some cases but not in others is *prudential*. Now in much discussion of international relations, prudential reasons are usually regarded as alternatives to moral ones. Moral reasons are supposed to operate in terms of the principle of absolute duty, which obliges heroic action that disdains the calculating concern for consequences. By comparison prudential reasons seem selfish and grubby, native to the discourse of merchants, not of moral heroes. Such suppositions, however, express a particular view of morality that is indebted to Immanuel Kant (although, in my view, it owes less to Kant than it thinks). There are other views, however. One of these stems from the Christian thought of Thomas Aquinas, and has generated the doctrine of justified war. In the Thomistic tradition of ethics, as in much classical Greek and Roman thought, prudence is a virtue. It is not the only virtue, and it is not the only or primary consideration in moral deliberation, but it is one of them. Applied to cases where military intervention is under consideration, prudence forbids action that is likely to be disproportionate—that is, where the means subverts the end, or where the good that one aims to secure looks set to be overwhelmed by the evils incurred in securing it. The moral virtue of prudence and its offspring, the criterion of proportionality, therefore, help to justify the difference between N.A.T.O.'s responses to Chechnya and Kosovo. Had N.A.T.O. intervened in Chechnya in 1994–96 or in 1999–2000 it would certainly have provoked war with Russia, thereby risking escalation to the point of an exchange of nuclear weapons. While it would have been good to save Chechen civilians from indiscriminate and

---

31. Crawshaw, "A Journey into the Unknown," 15.

disproportionate injury by Russian troops, it is reasonable to argue that it would not have been proportionate to do so at the risk of nuclear war. By contrast, there was no serious risk of direct war with Russia, and so of nuclear escalation, in the case of Kosovo. Yes, Russia had cultural and political interests in Serbia, which motivated her support of the Milošević regime; but her interests were not so vital as to make it likely that she would go to war with N.A.T.O. in defence of them.

The third kind of moral reason that can warrant different behaviour in different cases is *political*. If any regime is to go to war and stay at war, it must be able to win and maintain popular support. This is especially so in the case of democracies, but not only so. Even a regime as undemocratic as that of Tsar Nicholas II proved unable to sustain either war against Germany or its own survival in the face of overwhelming popular dissent. After all, it is invariably the people who must fill the uniforms of the soldiers that a regime would send to war; and if sufficient of the people object to a war strongly enough, then the regime can neither begin nor continue to prosecute it. This is certainly a practical, political consideration; but how is it moral? It is moral insofar as the *raison d'être* of any regime is its service of the good of its own people; and while it is quite possible that a regime might have a better grasp of that good than the people themselves, there nevertheless comes a point where, having failed to convince, a regime is morally obliged to defer to the popular will. Accordingly, one reason why the British Government intervened in Afghanistan in 2001 was its ability to win the support of a large majority of the British electorate. It is very unlikely that it would have won similar support for direct intervention on the same scale in Darfur.

VI. Why National Interest Need Not Be Selfish

This brings us to the issue of national interest. In the popular Kantian view of international ethics, national interest is assumed to be an *im*moral motive. Therefore, the fact that such interests helped to motivate Britain's interventions in Kosovo and Iraq is usually held to count against their moral justification. I regard this view of morality as mistaken, and I prefer the alternative provided by the ethical tradition stemming from Aquinas. Combining the opening chapters of the biblical book of Genesis with Aristotle, Thomist thought does not view all self-interest as selfish and immoral. Indeed, it holds that there is such a thing as morally obligatory self-love. The human individual has a duty to care for him- or herself properly, to seek what is genuinely his or her own good. As with an individual, so with a national community and the organ of its cohesion and decision, namely, its government: a national government has a moral duty to look after the well being of its own people—and in that sense to advance its genuine interests. Such a duty is not unlimited, of course. There cannot be a moral duty to pursue the interests of one's own nation by riding roughshod over the rights of others. Still, not every pursuit of national interest does perpetrate injustice, and so the fact that national interests are among the motives for military intervention does not by itself vitiate the latter's moral justification.

This is politically important, because some kind of national interest needs to be involved if military intervention is to attract popular support. One such interest can be moral integrity. Nations usually want to believe that they are doing the right or the noble thing, and they will tolerate the costs of war—up to a point—in a just cause that looks set to succeed. I have yet to meet a Briton who is not proud of what British troops achieved in Sierra Leone in the year 2000, even though Britain had no material stake in the outcome of that country's civil war, and even though intervention there cost British taxpayers money and British families casualties.[32] Citizens care that their country should do the right thing.

The nation's interest in its own moral integrity and nobility alone, however, will probably not underwrite military intervention that incurs very heavy costs. So other interests—such as national security—are needed to stiffen popular support for a major intervention. In the case of Kosovo, for example, Britain did have a security interest, albeit not immediate, in the stability of the Balkans, and therefore in curbing the activity of the Serbian source of recent disturbance. But note that this national interest was not private to Britain. It was shared by the other European members of N.A.T.O., and by the Balkan peoples themselves. Indeed, it was also shared by the U.N., whose Security Council had adopted Resolutions (1160, 1199, and 1203) in 1998, which legally bound the Federal Republic of Yugoslavia to cease all action by its security forces affecting the civilian population of Kosovo; to withdraw all security units used for civilian repression; and to implement in full all agreements with N.A.T.O. and the Organization for Security and Cooperation in Europe. These, together with statements

---

32. The British casualties were very light: one dead, one seriously injured, and twelve wounded (www.eliteukforces.info/special-air-service/sas-operations/operation-barras/, accessed on 24 November 2009).

following the Račak massacre in January 1999, judged that the government in Belgrade had created a humanitarian emergency in Kosovo that constituted a threat to peace and security in the Balkans.[33]

The presence of national interest as a motive need not vitiate military intervention. Not all interests are avaricious. One of them is moral integrity itself; for nations care about being right, and not only about being secure and fat. But even a nation's interest in its own security—or more exactly, even a national government's concern for the security of millions of fellow-countrymen—need not be private; for one nation's security is often bound up with others' security. As Gareth Evans puts it: "these days, good international citizenship is a matter of national self-interest."[34]

So national interest need not vitiate intervention. More than this, however, some kind of interest will be necessary to enable it. For it is not unreasonable for a national people to ask why they should bear the burdens of military intervention, especially in remote parts of the world. It is not unreasonable for them to ask why *they* should bear the burdens *rather than* others. It is not unreasonable for them to ask why *their* sons and daughters should suffer and die. And the answer to those reasonable questions will have to present itself in terms of the nation's own interests. And it could and ought to present itself in terms of the nation's own morally legitimate interests.

VII. How to Break the Law Responsibly

Anxieties about unchecked tyranny apart, it would be ideal if there were a global government with a global police force, which could act impartially and efficiently to uphold international law by stopping criminal acts, arresting those responsible, and bringing them to court. It would be ideal, if there were a cosmopolis. We are, however, a long way from the ideal; and I, for one, am sceptical that we will ever realize it.

Why am I sceptical? Because it seems to me that moral and political norms across the globe are too diverse, and international mistrust is accordingly too great, to permit the degree of consensus required for comprehensive legal specification of state crimes and for impartial and efficient

---

33. Resolutions 1199 and 1203 both speak of "impending humanitarian catastrophe" and assert that the situation in Kosovo "constitutes a threat to peace and security in the region."

34. Evans, *The Responsibility to Protect*, 144.

enforcement of international law. Maybe in time moral and political consensus will grow, but I suspect that we are talking of centuries rather than decades. And even so, a measure of moral and political agreement does not yet amount to a single judicial and policing system. In Europe such national systems were imposed, sometimes coercively, by strong royal central government. Yes, the history of the formation of the federal United States and of the confederal European Union suggests that judicial and policing coherence can be negotiated, and need not always be coerced. However, in the case of the U.S. such negotiation was made possible by a very high degree of cultural homogeneity and by the short histories of the individual constituent colonies. The much longer histories of the member states of the E.U., and their much more limited cultural similarity, has meant that the process of unification has been much more prolonged and might never be as complete. In the absence of a single state that is able and willing to force and sustain (over centuries) a comprehensively global empire, we can expect that the deep cultural differences between the West and the likes of China, India, and even Russia—differences that have been entrenched by centuries and even millennia of largely separate historical development—will continue to hinder agreement on what sovereign states should not be allowed to do, on the creation of a standing global police force, and on the delegation of enforcement to it.

For the foreseeable future, then, we will remain in our current situation. This is one where, on the one hand, many nations (such as China and India) continue to insist that *only* the Security Council may authorize military intervention, and that only directly authorized intervention is legal. They insist on this because they do not trust the grounds on which others might want to intervene, because they fear that they themselves might become subject to such intervention, and because they therefore want to control it as much as they can. On the other hand, there are other nations who are not content with an international system that allows the politics of the Security Council, and especially the casting of a veto, to stymie effective action, sometimes military, against a state's grossly atrocious behaviour. The recent fate of *The Responsibility to Protect* report in international debate gives no ground for hope that this crucial point of disagreement is going to be resolved any time soon.[35]

What, then, are we to do in the long meantime? I suggest the following. It is far preferable that the Security Council should authorize effective

---

35. See Bellamy, *Responsibility to Protect*.

Sovereignty and Responsibility

action to punish states that are guilty of gross atrocities. Such authorization carries maximal international authority and is beyond suspicion of being motivated primarily by private and illegitimate national interests. Therefore any state that would see gross atrocities punished, and which cares to maintain the authority of international law, should do its utmost to secure Security Council authorization. However, if the Security Council is not able to authorize the enforcement of international law, then states may intervene militarily without authorization, provided that they meet the conditions of moral justification articulated earlier. If they meet those conditions, then such intervention will intend the goals of the international community as expressed by the U.N., albeit not by its preferred means; and it will be multilateral, not unilateral. For sure, this kind of unauthorized intervention might weaken the authority of international law; but that must be weighed against the fact that the Security Council's inability to enforce the law has already weakened it, and that its successful blocking of remedial action would weaken it even further.

How far unauthorized action will weaken it depends on how successful are the intervening states in persuading others of their case.[36] States that fear international intervention, should they ever embark on genocide and its like, will of course never be persuaded. Others, however, might be. Take the case of Kosovo. There the Security Council had been unable to authorize N.A.T.O.'s intervention because Russia threatened to cast its veto. However, when Russia subsequently proposed a Resolution condemning the intervention, the Council refused by a vote of twelve to three. N.A.T.O.'s action, then, was at once *not expressly authorized* and yet *expressly not condemned* by a majority of four to one. When the Security Council itself refuses to condemn unauthorized intervention by such a margin, is it not reasonable to infer that an overwhelming majority of the international community has been persuaded of the necessity, the public-spiritedness, and the proportionality of the action? What is more, such action has not actually set a precedent for rogue states to ride roughshod over international law. And if that is so, then how exactly has the law's authority been weakened at all?[37]

36. Thus Gareth Evans: "The effectiveness of the global collective security system, as with any other legal order, depends ultimately not only on the legality of decisions but also on *the common perception of their legitimacy*: their being made on solid evidentiary grounds, for the right reasons, morally as well as legally" (*The Responsibility to Protect*, 139. My emphasis.).

37. I note that Gareth Evans reaches a conclusion that is close to my own: "While it is obviously optimal for any military action to be both unquestionably legal under

VIII. Conclusion

National sovereignty should be seen as the freedom to incarnate and develop human goods in creative ways appropriate to particular circumstances. It should not be seen as a state's moral licence to do as it pleases within its own borders, and to ignore what happens outside of them. This is because the exercise of national sovereignty is responsible to created natural law, which—following Hugo Grotius and diverging from Thomas Hobbes—springs partly from a primordial sense of social duty. National sovereigns, therefore, have moral obligations not to oppress their own peoples and, all other things being equal, to rescue foreign peoples from grave domestic oppression. Nevertheless, given the possibility of unilateral self-delusion and manipulation, and absent any anxieties about global tyranny, it would be best if military intervention for humanitarian purposes were directed by a universal sovereign state—a cosmopolis—with an impartial concern for the common, global good. Sadly, perhaps, we do not have that, and nor are we likely to achieve it any time soon. Instead, what we have is law that reserves the authorization of humanitarian intervention to a body, the United Nations' Security Council, whose capacity to act is at the mercy of a single veto, which may be cast for reasons of irresponsible national self-interest. Should the Security Council be hamstrung in such a situation, moral obligation might trump legal requirement: it might be morally right to break the law. While it is true that unauthorized action might damage the law's authority, it is no less true that failure to enforce the law against gross and massive violations of human rights does damage it. Whether unauthorized military action also damages the law's authority depends on the view that comes to prevail among the international community. And that depends on factors such as these: the earnestness with which the agent of unauthorized intervention sought (in vain) the Security Council's blessing; how far the intervention's aims, as distinct from its means, are consonant with those of the U.N.; how multilateral is the agent; how grave and persistent the injustice to be remedied; and how proportionate the means of remedy. How far transgression of the law's letter damages its authority hangs crucially upon the manner of its transgression.

---

international law and more or less universally accepted as legitimate (as was the case, for example, with the 1991 Gulf War), it is fair to suggest that military action that is technically illegal but widely perceived to be legitimate (as with Kosovo in 1999) does far less damage than action which is generally perceived to be neither legal nor legitimate (Iraq in 2003)" (*Responsibility to Protect*, 139).

4

Nationalism and Empire

I. Getting behind "Imperialism"

There was a time when many people, at least in Europe, thought that empire was a good thing, bringing the benefits of modern technological efficiency, as well as scientific, moral, and religious enlightenment, to the benighted places and peoples of the earth. Those of us whose parents were born before 1914 are separated from that era by a single generation. By the end of the First World War, however, several mighty stars in the imperial firmament had fallen and the future of those that remained looked insecure. Moreover, the sheer fact of imperial dissolution—whether Ottoman or Austro-Hungarian or German or Russian—was given moral impetus, when, at the 1919 Paris Peace Conference, Woodrow Wilson lent American weight to the notion that nations possess a right to self-determination. Since then empires have invariably been identified with imperialism, and the benefit of doubt has rested heavily on the side of nationalist movements for the creation of independent nation-states.

The distinction between nation-state and empire, however, is not as clear as is commonly assumed. The United Kingdom, for example, is a multi-national state created in part by England's conquest of Wales and Ireland in the medieval and early modern periods. (Scotland was never conquered, but chose union with England in 1707.) Insofar as "empire" means the annexation of foreign territory, therefore, today's nation-state of the U.K. is partly the offspring of English empire. The same applies, *mutatis mutandis*, to France. Even the United States of America, notwithstanding its birth in a struggle for independence from British imperial constraints, made itself an empire by annexing territory inhabited (if not settled) by native Americans west of the Appalachian mountains.

Nation-states and empires are not always distinct in the manner of their self-constitution. Nor are they always distinct morally. If empires have presided over atrocities, so have nation-states. It is true that the British empire presided over the brutal suppression of the Mau-Mau rebellion in 1952–60. But it is also true that the U.S.A. has on its conscience the massacre at Wounded Knee in 1890; Germany, the Holocaust in the 1940s; and the People's Republic of China, the Great Leap Forward in the 1950s.

While the vices of empire have dominated later twentieth-century consciousness, some wistful awareness of its virtues revived in the 1990s. The implosion of the Yugoslav Federation into nasty, brutal civil war between rival nationalists—Christian Bosnians and Muslim Bosnians, Catholic Croats and Orthodox Serbs, Orthodox Serbs and Muslim Kosovars—highlighted the virtue of trans-national order, even when coerced by a central authority, in enabling diverse peoples or nations to live together in peace. The same thought surfaces when one contemplates the post-1919 history of the Middle East. During the First World War, the Ottoman empire was widely regarded (at least in Britain) as corruptly repressive and ripe for dismantling, and no doubt it was. But here we are, almost a century later, still reeling from the distant after-shocks of its dissolution, and baffled over how to settle things—forever in Israel-Palestine, recently in Iraq, and now in Syria.

In this final chapter, therefore, I want to get behind the essentializing idea of imperialism and reflect on the varied reality of the imperial phenomenon, to argue that empire is no less morally complex and ambiguous than nation, to identify what can be right with it and what tends to go wrong with it, and to argue that justice does not always lie with those nationalists who want to secede from it. This is a huge topic, and all that I can hope to do here is make a beginning.

II. Is the Bible Anti-empire?

1. Norman Gottwald on the Old Testament

As a Christian ethicist, I am bound to take my bearings, in the first place, from biblical tradition. As it happens, during the last fifteen years the topic

Nationalism and Empire

of empire has increasingly commanded the attention of scholars of the Bible, and especially of the New Testament, as the titles of the following books testify: Richard Horsley's *Paul and Empire* (1997), Warren Carter's *Matthew and Empire* (2001), Horsley's *Jesus and Empire: The Kingdom of God and the New World Disorder* (2003), John Dominic Crossan and Jonathan L. Reed's *In Search of Paul: How' Jesus Apostle Opposed Rome's Empire with God's Kingdom* (2005), and Neil Elliott's *The Arrogance of Nations: Reading Romans in the Shadow of Empire* (2008).[1] It is not a coincidence that every one of the authors that I have just cited lives and works in America, since the reason for this recent focus is not hard to discern: namely, the emergence of the United States as the sole superpower after 1989. The moral assumption that informs these scholars' biblical interpretation is that empire is, basically, wrong. The interpretative conclusion that they reach is that the Bible, and especially the New Testament, says that empire is, basically, wrong. Thus their implicit, and sometimes not-so-implicit, moral-political conclusion is that, insofar as one regards the Bible's moral views to be authoritative, the imperial foreign policy of the administration of George W. Bush was wrong.

I am going to argue that this set of assumption, interpretation, and conclusion is considerably mistaken; and I will do so primarily by analyzing some of the essays in another collection edited by Richard Horsley, *In the Shadow of Empire: Reclaiming the Bible as a History of Faithful Resistance* (2008).

I begin with Norman Gottwald's chapter, which is entitled, "Early Israel as an Anti-Imperial Community." In its third sentence Gottwald asserts that "[e]mpires, both ancient and modern, impose systems of domination parasitically on subject peoples."[2] For historical grounding of this definition he points to the political economy of the empires of the ancient Near-East. There the rulers of centralized imperial states granted the peasantry, composing 98 percent of the populace, only the right of land-*use*, while reserving for themselves the right to tax its produce by demanding tribute.[3] Gottwald's thesis is that "[e]arly Israel was born as an anti-imperial

---

1. In his contribution to Horsley's *Jesus and Empire* Neil Elliott writes that "[s]ince the 1990s, interpreters have increasingly sought to understand the apostle Paul in the context of Roman imperial culture. This surge of interest is part of a new awareness of the role of empire in biblical studies generally, of which this volume is one expression" ("The Apostle Paul and Empire," 97).

2. Gottwald, "Early Israel as an Anti-Imperial Community," 9.

3. Ibid., 9–10.

resistance movement that broke away from Egyptian and Canaanite domination to become a self-governing community of free peasants . . . that provided dignity and livelihood for all members of the community."[4] The biblical story of the exodus from Egypt and the conquest of Canaan he judges historically implausible. Nevertheless, it is to be taken seriously as "a symbolic projection . . . [of] Israel's exiting, going forth, from imperial oppression in Canaan . . . and of Israel's coming to independent self-rule in the highland territories of Canaan."[5] That is to say, the early Israelites were never actually slaves in Egypt, they never left, and they never conquered Canaan. Instead, they were peasants who threw off the tributary oppression of the city-dwelling Canaanites, who were themselves Egyptian vassals, and set up independent communities in the highlands.[6] The social and political structure of these communities was "anti-hierarchic" and so "anti-imperialist," amounting to a form of decentralized "regulated anarchy."[7] Eventually, however, the threat posed to their independence by the Philistines moved the Israelites to appoint Saul as commander-in-chief. Thus began a gradual process of political centralization, which led to the oppressive regime of Solomon. "This," Gottwald assures us, "was not an inevitable process, but one that seems to have unfolded without any of the participants being fully aware of where it was leading."[8] After adopting kingship under David and Solomon, the Israelites too ended up participating in the tributary political economy, and, Gottwald admits, there are "strands of the biblical literature [that] are supportive of the tributary system, and even celebrate it, principally the texts that praise the just rule of kings, in sharp contrast to the dismal record of kingship recorded in the books of Kings." However, he assures us that "[m]ore often . . . the biblical witnesses turn the anger and justice of God against the tributary injustices, which the deity will punish sooner or later."[9] Gottwald follows his reconstruction of the history of early

---

4. Ibid., 9.

5. Ibid., 16–17.

6. Ibid., 13, 17. What Gottwald is doing here is assimilating the early Israelites to the "socially and politically marginalised people, known as *habiru* or *apiru*" (ibid., 14). He acknowledges that this "remains a matter of continuing discussion" and that "no direct line of continuity is traceable from the Amarna *habiru* to the early Israelites 150 years later." Nevertheless, he thinks it "reasonable to hypothesize" that a fair number of Israelites were of *habiru* descent (ibid., 14–15).

7. Ibid., 17–18.

8. Ibid., 20.

9. Ibid., 12–13.

Israel with a concluding section entitled, "Implications for the American Empire." Here, drawing an analogy between past and present, he argues that "in a supreme irony, Palestinians of the West Bank may most nearly approximate the early Israelites since they occupy the same terrain, practice similar livelihoods, and long for deliverance from the 'Canaanite' state of Israel backed by the American empire."[10]

I agree with Gottwald's concluding analogy, but I disagree with most of what precedes it. One point of disagreement is over what empires have been historically, and therefore what they can be. Gottwald might well be correct in his morally critical description of ancient Near Eastern empires as grossly unequal and oppressive of the vast majority. However, to sum up all empires everywhere and all of the time simply as systems of domination parasitic on subject peoples is, I think, historically untrue. I shall say more about that before the end of this chapter.

My most basic objection to Gottwald's essay is methodological. On the surface it might appear that Gottwald is appealing to the authority of the Bible, in order to establish the moral normativity of anti-imperialism. In fact, however, he is not actually doing that, since what is authoritative for him is not the text itself, but the history that he claims to find *behind*, and sometimes *in spite of*, the text. Yet that still does not quite capture the truth of the situation, because history as a bare, descriptive chronology of what happened in the past cannot be morally authoritative in itself. So what Gottwald is actually doing is bringing his already settled moral convictions about imperialism to the text, rejecting those parts of it that contradict them, and then reconstructing early Israelite history in their light. Since nothing in the text itself is allowed to resist his assumptions, and cause him to reflect critically on them, the text itself exercises no moral authority. It merely provides passive matter for his moral assumptions to act upon—and that, of course, raises the question of why Gottwald bothers at all with the biblical text in the first place.

In contrast to Gottwald's method, I believe that an approach that regards the biblical text as authoritative needs to be more dialectical. It needs to heed the text's discordant voices, to try and discern what can be true on both sides, and to work its way to a synthesis. In the process some elements of both thesis and antithesis might well be dropped, because they are deemed to be inconsistent with the emerging synthesis. So the synthesizing process will be critical, and the criteria will issue from the moral

---

10. Ibid., 24.

assumptions of the interpreter. However, in this dialectical process, the text will be permitted to have a formative influence on those assumptions. So, for example, take the tension—maybe contradiction—between the "prophetic" and the "monarchist" strands in the Old Testament. The prophetic strand takes a very dim view indeed of the exploitation of the poor by the rich and powerful, while the monarchist strand extols the virtues of the Davidic monarchy. Gottwald's response is simply to dismiss the latter as morally corrupt, for he *knows* that hierarchy is necessarily oppressive. My alternative is to claim that *both* of the strands contain truths that are, as all truth ultimately has to be, mutually consistent. On the one hand, it is true that political centralization and its attendant hierarchy can foster the evil of social oppression. On the other hand, it can also secure the good of political security from foreign enemies and from domestic criminals—a good without which no other social goods can flourish. The empirical, historical truth is that a weak centre renders the members of a political community vulnerable, which is precisely why centralization tends to happen. *Pace* Gottwald, I think that the exigencies of political survival made Israel's centralization practically inevitable. But is it possible to enjoy centralization's security without inviting its oppression? Yes it is. Centres can regard themselves as holding their privileges only as servants of the periphery. Heads can regard themselves as no more important than feet to the flourishing of the whole. Certainly, St. Paul thought so, when in 1 Corinthians 12 he used the metaphor of the body to describe proper social relations within the church. A body *does* have a head and feet; it *is* hierarchical. Hierarchy is not the issue. The issue, rather, is how those at the top regard themselves, and therefore how they regard and treat those at the bottom. Had Gottwald paused to listen to the biblical text, instead of just using it for his own prefabricated purposes, he might have learned that.

III. Is the Bible Anti-empire?

2. Richard Horsley on Jesus

The second and third essays in Richard Horsley's collection that I want to examine are by Horsley himself: his "Introduction: The Bible and Empires" and his chapter on "Jesus and Empire." The shadow of Iraq falls heavily across both of them. Horsley tells us that only after the 2003 invasion "did more than a handful of biblical interpreters begin to question the received

Nationalism and Empire

wisdom" that Jesus was apolitical, and to discover his anti-imperialist agenda;[11] and using terms that reportage from Iraq has made familiar, he describes Herod's sending forth troops to massacre the innocents as a Roman client king's dispatch of "counterinsurgency" forces,[12] and he tells us that Jesus was crucified as an "insurgent leader."[13] Although he never says so directly, Horsley makes it implicitly clear that he regards the invasion of Iraq as an imperialist act and by definition wrong. It was the latest expression of the United States' sinful aspiration to become the New Rome, extending the rule of law over uncivilized peoples, if need be by force of arms.[14] As such it was also the latest betrayal of America's original, pristine identity as the New Israel, who escaped "the pharaoh-like tyranny of English monarchs" in general and "the tyrannical rule of George III" in particular.[15]

It is quite obvious, therefore, that when Horsley turns to the text of the New Testament, he does so with certain moral assumptions already firmly in place: empire *is* tyranny and therefore wrong. His thesis is that Jesus' mission belonged to the Galilean tradition of direct opposition to the Roman empire.[16] In support of this he offers several arguments, among them the following. First, the stories of Jesus' exorcisms should be read in the light of ethnographic studies of demon possession among East African peoples, in whose "exorcism cults the names of some of the demons were of invasive foreign forces, such as 'Lord Cromer' (the British general who led the military expedition south through the Sudan)."[17] Accordingly, the story in the Gospel of Mark (5:1–20) about the exorcism of "Legion" should be read as a symbolic expulsion of Roman troops.[18] Second, Mark's story (12:13–17) about Jesus' response to the Pharisees' and Herodians' trick-question about the legality of paying tribute to Caesar should also be read in anti-imperialist terms, since his audience would have understood quite

11. Horsley, "Jesus and Empire," 77. Certainly, the thesis that Jesus espoused radical politics was not first formulated after the Iraq invasion. At least as far back as the rebellious 1960s scholars such as S. G. F. Brandon were arguing that Jesus should be seen as a political revolutionary. See, for example, *Jesus and the Zealots*.
12. Horsley, "Introduction: The Bible and Empires," 7.
13. Ibid., 5.
14. Ibid., 3, 5.
15. Ibid., 1; Horsley, "Jesus and Empire," 96.
16. Horsley, "Introduction," 5; Horsley, "Jesus and Empire," 95.
17. Horsley, "Jesus and Empire," 85.
18. Ibid., 86.

clearly that *all* things belong to God for the support of God's people: "While couched in a clever circumlocution, Jesus' answer was still a blunt declaration of the people's independence of Roman imperial rule/kingdom, since they belonged directly under the rule/kingdom of God."[19] Similarly, third, Jesus' condemnation of the Temple and the priestly rulers of Jerusalem was anti-Roman, since both were instruments of Roman rule in general and of tribute-collection in particular.[20] Fourth and finally, in that Jesus "had the audacity to march up to Jerusalem at the highly charged time of Passover, carry out a forcible demonstration symbolizing God's condemnation of the Temple, and state, however cleverly, that it was not lawful to render tribute to Caesar," he confronted the Roman governor and the client-rulers of Jerusalem with acts of insurrection that they "could not tolerate."[21] He was therefore crucified as an insurgent against Roman rule.[22] Horsley's conclusion is this: that the United States should follow Jesus, repent of its imperialist ways, and return to its original position in the Israelite tradition of resistance to "Empire."[23]

I do not doubt that Jesus' teaching and conduct had—and has—political import. Nor do I wish to quarrel with the claim that he was critical of Roman conduct. What I do resist, however, is the representation of the politics of Jesus, and of his earliest followers, as "anti-empire." It is telling that at one point Horsley refers to "Empire" with a capital "E." What this indicates is that he thinks that all actual empires share the same basic nature, that empire always and everywhere means essentially the same thing: tyranny. I think that this is wrong. I think that empirically, historically "empire" can mean significantly different things at different times and places. Indeed, if the British empire is anything to go by, then "empire" can mean significantly different things *at the same time* in different places. And when I say "significant," I mean "morally significant." Unlike Horsley (and Gottwald), I do not think that empire is always and everywhere wicked, nor that nationalist resistance is always and everywhere just. One must judge case by case, first *looking* at what is happening, and only then formulating a judgement. When we do that, we will often find a moral complexity that crude talk of "imperialism" and "anti-imperialism" glibly passes over.

19. Ibid., 90.
20. Ibid., 79–80, 91, 93.
21. Ibid., 95.
22. Ibid., 75.
23. Ibid., 96.

Nationalism and Empire

Take, for example, the secession of the American colonies from the British empire. On this Horsley is, ironically, an American conservative, unthinkingly endorsing nationalist myth, which nourishes the bias of his biblical interpretation. By "myth" here I do not mean something simply untrue, but rather a simplistic rendering of the truth—a half-truth. According to the American myth, the war of 1775–83 was one of "freedom" against "tyranny." What was the tyranny supposedly at issue? Answer: monarchy with absolutist, unconstitutional tendencies, manifested in the arbitrary imposition of intolerable taxes, and enforced by brutal military coercion. Here we have the imperialist archetype of empire. But is this an accurate description of the actual behaviour of George III and British government? Or is this archetype in fact a stereotype? It is true that Whig politicians in Britain believed that the king was subverting the Constitution by using royal patronage to control (buy) Parliament, and that this reading of events influenced their *confrères* in colonial America. It is true that in 1765 the Grenville ministry unilaterally imposed direct taxation upon the colonies, which was unprecedented, by way of the Stamp Act.[24] It is true that the American colonists did not have direct representation in Westminster. And it is true that the behaviour of British troops in and around Boston on the eve of war was sometimes provocative and sometimes brutal.

All that is true; but the following is also true. First, contemporary historians judge that Whig anxiety about another resurgence of absolute monarchy in England was altogether overwrought: the buying of political influence by the Crown was a serious problem, but it fell a long way short of what the word "tyranny" connotes. (And, one might point out, the buying of political influence—by private individuals and commercial corporations—is something that many contemporary Americans seem entirely untroubled by.) Second, the Townsend taxes had been levied to help defray the costs of the French and Indian War of 1754–63, which had secured the English colonies in America, but had resulted in a doubling of the British national debt and a quintupling of the expense of colonial defence and administration.[25] Nevertheless, thanks to a combination of American resistance (including mob violence), British mercantile lobbying, and a change of ministry, the Stamp Act was repealed the following year. Besides, that issue rose and fell nine years before the outbreak of war in 1775. The infamous customs duty on tea that did precipitate war was quite different: it

24. Reynolds, *America, Empire of Liberty*, 58.
25. Ibid., 56.

was an "external" tax, the likes of which had long been used by the imperial government to raise revenue. Third, while it is true that the colonies did not elect Members of Parliament to Westminster, they did have agents in London, who recruited British M.P.s to their cause. American views were not unrepresented; and even if they had been represented directly, they would not necessarily have prevailed. And fourth, eighteenth-century soldiery was generally unruly and brutal: come the war, even American patriots did atrocious things. Yet the most famous instance of British military brutality is surely the "Boston Massacre," when bloodthirsty redcoats gunned down innocent civilians—except that, as historians now acknowledge, the redcoats weren't so bloodthirsty, nor the civilians so innocent.

To this picture, three further factors need to be added. First, as became clear during the French and Indian War, there was a significant cultural gap between the American colonists and their British cousins. The latter came from a society in which aristocrats expected and received a measure of deference from their social inferiors. The former came from a society composed of a much higher proportion of self-made people, especially independent farmers, to whom social deference did not come naturally.[26] Second, one of the manifestations of "tyranny" against which the colonists reacted was the British granting of religious tolerance to Roman Catholics in Quebec in the Quebec Act of 1774. Roman Catholicism being equated with political tyranny, this was taken as a further sign of the absolutist tendencies of British government. In fact, it was nothing of the sort. The granting of tolerance was merely an act of political prudence (and none the worse for that), aimed at encouraging the Catholic French to live peaceably under British rule. Third and finally, in the aftermath of the French and Indian War, the British had promised native Americans that colonists would not invade and settle the lands west of the Appalachians. To the colonists, of course, this was another manifestation of "tyranny"—a deeply unwelcome constraint upon what they saw as their natural right to expand. Urging the claims of the United States upon the Mississippi valley against Spain, James Madison, the chief architect of the U.S. Constitution, wrote to Lafayette in 1785:

> Nature has given the use of the Mississippi to those who may settle on its waters, as she gave the United States their independence.... Nature seems on all sides to be reasserting those rights which have so long been trampled on by tyranny and bigotry.... If the United

26. This is Fred Anderson's thesis in *Crucible of War*.

Nationalism and Empire

States were to become parties to the occlusion of the Mississippi they would be guilty of treason against the very laws under which they obtained and hold their national existence.[27]

On the natural rights of the native Americans, of course, Madison was absolutely silent.

That, then, is the more morally complicated history of the war by which the American colonies seceded from the British empire. To summarize that conflict as a battle between colonial "liberty" and imperial "tyranny" does not begin to do the details justice, and it misleads far more than it informs. Yes, the imperial centre was remote, both in miles and increasingly in culture. Yes, the representation of the colonists and their interests in the imperial law-making and tax-imposing parliament was only indirect, and so weaker than it could (and arguably should) have been. But the principle that the primary beneficiaries of the French and Indian War should bear a fair share of its costs is incontrovertible; and the practice of "external" taxation by which the Government sought to realize that principle had long been established. What is more, in this case it was the *empire* that upheld the *liberty* of Roman Catholics to practice their religion in Quebec, and the *liberty* of native Americans not to be invaded—and the empire upheld these liberties against the colonial anti-imperialists. Empires do not always live down to their stereotypes, any more than "freedom-fighters" always live up to theirs.

The same point applies to Horsley's invocation of East African exorcism cults, and serves to undermine his argument. He gives two examples of imperialist demons regularly cast out, and in one case at least his choice is most unfortunate. He refers, you will remember, to demons representing "invasive foreign forces, such as 'Lord Cromer' (the British general who led the military expedition south through the Sudan)."[28] This example is unhelpful to his argument in two respects. First of all, Lord Cromer was not a general, but a banker then administrator. His name was Evelyn Baring (as in Barings Bank). When the Egyptian government became unable to finance its debts in the late 1870s—partly because it couldn't persuade large landowners to pay anything but light taxes—the khedive sought loans from Europe. France and Britain agreed a bail-out, but only on condition that they oversee the reform of the Egyptian government's finances (rather as the European Union has behaved toward Greece and Italy during the

---

27. Ketcham, *James Madison*, 177. See also pp. 96–97.
28. Horsley, "Jesus and Empire," 85.

recent financial crisis in the eurozone). Evelyn Baring was sent to Cairo to design and implement the reforms. Naturally, the Egyptian ruling classes felt humiliated, and they resented Baring's undoubtedly autocratic manner. Baring did not have a very high opinion of Egyptian government officials in general—any more than his contemporary counterparts have of Afghan ones. Consequently, Baring did become a hate-figure among anti-imperialists. His biographer tells of the local archivist in the Norfolk town of Cromer being approached by some Egyptian students in 1998, who asked him where Lord Cromer is buried. He told them what they wanted to know, but then expressed himself curious as to the motives of their visit. They replied, "We would like to spit on his grave"[29] So he was not popular among nationalists. But was he a wicked tyrant? Not obviously. Certainly Baring himself was quite convinced that his reforms were in the interests of the native *fellahin* or peasants, and that he cared for them far more than the middle-class nationalists clamouring for freedom from quasi-imperial rule. How right or wrong he was, an economist would have to tell you. But I find it hard to quarrel with his motive, his intention, or his twenty-five year commitment.

Horsley's choice of imperialist demon is unfortunate in a second respect, too. Lord Cromer was not the general who led British and Egyptian troops up the Nile from Egypt into the Sudan. That was Herbert Kitchener. And what was Kitchener doing invading the Sudan? He was doing the bidding of a Gladstone government that had, with the deepest reluctance, bowed to popular pressure and ordered an army to go to the rescue of General Charles George ("Chinese") Gordon. Why did Gordon need rescuing? Because he was besieged in Khartoum by the Islamist forces of the Mahdi. And what was Gordon doing in Khartoum, and what made certain Sudanese seriously unhappy at his presence? Gordon, a very convinced Christian, was intent upon suppressing the slave-trade. *Pace* Horsley, empire is not always imperialist; and anti-imperialists are not, by definition, just.

The moral and political assumptions that Horsley brings to the biblical text are dubious, and his interpretation of it is correspondingly distorted. Jesus, he tells us, was opposed to the Roman empires, and that is why the imperialist Romans had him killed. The weakness of the evidence adduced in support of this interpretation, however, exposes its tendentiousness. Horsley's anti-Roman reading of the story of the exorcism of the Gerasene demoniac, for example, rests entirely on the meaning of the name that the

---

29. Owen, *Lord Cromer*, vii.

possessing evil spirit gives himself: "Legion" (Mark 5:9). This, of course, can refer to a Roman military unit comprising between five and six thousand Roman soldiers, but it can also be used as a metaphor for a large number of all sorts of things (as it is sometimes used in the English language). Words are not univocal. So how should we determine its meaning in this case? Are there are any other elements in the story *as told in the biblical text* that suggest a political, anti-Roman meaning? No, there are not. As Adela Yarbro Collins writes: "It may be that, in the original form of the account, the 'name' Legion was chosen to express an anti-Roman sentiment.... There is, however, no theme of opposition to Rome in Mark.... The aim of the story is not—at least not primarily—to make a statement about the Romans, but to show how Jesus rescued the man from his plight and restored him to a normal life."[30] What is more, the text itself tells us how to interpret the evil spirit's name. It tells us, "'My name is Legion,' he replied, 'for we are many'"—not, "My name is Legion, for we are Roman."

On the matter of Jesus' reply to the Pharisees' and Herodians' trick-question about paying tribute to Caesar, Horsley is, of course, quite right to say that his audience would have clearly understood that *all* things belong to God for the support of God's people. That, however, is beside the point. Unless one assumes, as some do, that the imposition of taxation by government *as such* contradicts God's ultimate ownership of all things, then the question arises of *when* taxation becomes a form of irresponsible stewardship. One answer that can find plenty of biblical and dominical support is that taxation is irresponsible when it is used for the benefit of the ruling few, and not that of the ruled many. Insofar as the Pharisees and Herodians assumed that view to be an implication of the injunction to give to God what belongs to God, and insofar as taxation in Palestine was of that kind, then we can read Jesus' reply as an oblique moral criticism of it—and of any taxation like it. But surely what is also significant about Jesus' response is that he refused to deny, as any nationalist Zealot would have done, the Roman empire's right to tax Jews at all. Instead, what he denied was anyone's right to tax in a manner inconsistent with God's equal love for all his creatures. That is to say, Jesus' concern was about the purpose of the taxation, not about the identity of the one taxing. His response was therefore even

---

30. Adela Yarbro Collins, *Mark*, 269–70. Collins' view is shared by other commentators of good repute, who find no political significance in the use of the name "Legion"—for example, William L. Lane in *The Gospel of Mark*; Robert Guelich in *Mark 1:1—8:26*; and Morna D. Hooker in *The Gospel according to St Mark*.

more radical than Horsley supposes, for it reached beyond the clichés of nationalist anti-imperialism to the moral root of the matter.

Similarly, the primary focus of Jesus' ire against the Temple cult was its rapacity, not the fact that it was ultimately backed by the Romans. That is why anti-Roman rhetoric is so strikingly absent in the Gospel texts: not because Jesus' original anti-imperialism had been air-brushed out by politically timorous Gospel writers, but because Jesus did not regard *empire* in itself as the root of political evil.

Finally, Horsley tells us that Jesus confronted the Roman governor and the client-rulers of Jerusalem with acts of insurrection that they "could not tolerate,"[31] and that he was therefore crucified as an insurgent against Roman rule.[32] However, as the Gospel texts actually tell the story, the prime movers of Jesus' death, if not its final executors, are the Jewish authorities. The Roman Governor, Pilate, appears very inclined to tolerate Jesus' activities until he is reluctantly manoeuvred into doing the will of the rabble-rousing chief priests and elders (Mark 15:1–15; Matt 27:11–26; Luke 23:1–25; John 18:28—19:16). The Gospels are unanimous in saying that Pilate considered Jesus to be *innocent* of the political charge against him (Matt 27:19, 23, 24; Mark 15:14a; Luke 23:14, 22; John 19:6b).

Of course, a biblical interpreter who is already a convinced anti-imperialist can always go behind the text to reconstruct the original, authentic, historical story of Jesus to suit his prejudices. However, given the paucity of supporting non-textual evidence, such a reconstruction is actually a highly speculative construction. And given that the historical construction contradicts the text, rather than interprets it, it has no right at all to such authority as the text itself possesses.

IV. Is the Bible Anti-empire?

3. Neil Elliott on Paul

To complete my coverage of the main elements in the Christian Bible, I turn now to Neil Elliott's essay, "The Apostle Paul and Empire." Unlike Gottwald and Horsley, Elliott's main strategy is not to discover a normative history behind the text, but rather to select a normative Paul out of it. Thus, he distinguishes the original, authentic Paul both from his later disciples, who,

---

31. Horsley, "Jesus and Empire," 95.
32. Ibid., 75.

in the likes of the Epistles to the Ephesians and Colossians, "accommodated the apostle's views to the dominant imperial order," and also from the picture drawn of him in the Act of the Apostles, where Luke presents him as "a model Roman citizen."[33] Elliott notes how, in his own letters, Paul "prides himself on how frequently he was hauled before civic magistrates and Roman officials, thrown into Roman prisons, and punished as a menace to public order—as proofs of his apostolic legitimacy."[34] The famous first seven verses of the thirteenth chapter of the Epistle to the Romans, however, throw Elliott momentarily off his anti-imperialist stride, since they belong to the authentically Pauline corpus and yet are "so uncharacteristically" Pauline. Their politically conservative affirmation of the beneficence of the governing authorities, and of the duty to be subject to them, stands "in stark contrast" to what Paul says elsewhere about the Roman order as "the present evil age," governed by "the rulers of this age, who are doomed to perish" (Gal 1:4; 1 Cor 2:6–8), and about looking forward to the "day of the Lord," which will bring the subjection and destruction of "every ruler and every authority and power" hostile to God (1 Cor 15:24–25). Elliott suggests that the anomaly of Romans 13 should be read in terms of Paul's dread of *anomia*, against which Roman force was sometimes a restraint, noting that some interpreters of the passage find in it a concern "to head off even the appearance of civic unrest in a politically volatile situation."[35] On one point Elliott does read the text in terms of what is behind it, when he gives Paul's proud insistence upon his ethnic identity an anti-colonial spin, by setting it against a background of imperial Roman contempt for the Jews.[36]

I do not doubt that Paul was critical, sometimes radically critical, of the Roman empire as he experienced it. What I do doubt is that his repudiation of Roman empire was any more wholesale than his affirmation of Jewish religion, and that his politics can be accurately summed-up as "anti-imperialist." If one assumes, as Elliott does, that when Paul refers to "the present evil age," he is speaking about the Roman imperial order as such, then his remarks in Romans 13:1–7 and his exercise of the Roman citizen's right to appeal to Caesar in Acts 25 do seem inconsistent. There is, however, nothing in the text of Galatians 1:4, or its immediate textual environment, that identifies "the present evil age" with Roman imperial

33. Elliott, "The Apostle Paul and Empire," 100.
34. Ibid.
35. Ibid., 110–12.
36. Ibid., 102, 103, 109.

order. In 1 Corinthians 2:6–8, Paul does contrapose the wisdom of God to that of the "rulers of this age," whom he identifies as those who "crucified the Lord of glory." Presumably by this Paul intended to refer to the Romans, but, unless his view of the causes of Jesus' death diverged sharply from that of the Gospels, he also intended to refer to the religious leaders of the Jews. Certainly, in the epistle's preceding chapter, Paul sets his gospel not only against the wisdom of the Greeks, but also against the expectations of the Jews. So what did the Roman and Jewish rulers of this age share—what was their common wisdom? Their "wisdom" was that the way of the cross, the way of weakness and lowliness, is foolish, whereas in fact it is the way of the power of God (1 Cor 1:18, 25). What this implies is that, in Paul's view, any social or political order—be it Roman or Jewish, imperial or religious—that is infused with un-Christian assumptions about power belongs to the evil age that is passing away. Whether Roman imperial order—and every other imperial order—*must* be so infused remains a moot point. Elliott assumes that it must be: imperial order is *necessarily* domineering and oppressive and abusive. Paul, however, appears not to share this view. As I have already mentioned, through his choice of a corporal metaphor for the evangelical community in 1 Corinthians 12, he claims that the root of social and political evil is not hierarchy as such, but the way in which those at the top overestimate themselves and underestimate their functional inferiors. And in Romans 13 he implies that Roman imperial authorities *can and sometimes do* use their coercive power for the purpose and in the manner for which God ordained it: to curb wrongdoing. As it happens, even Elliott himself inadvertently acknowledges that the Roman empire exhibited a measure of moral ambiguity. On the one hand, he tells us that the empire encouraged contempt toward subject peoples in general[37] and the Judaeans in particular.[38] And yet, on the other hand, he admits that Romans sometimes admired the Judaeans as an honourable "race of philosophers," and that

37. Ibid., 109. In writing of "the contemptuous attitude that the empire encouraged toward subject peoples" (ibid.), Elliott implies that racist contempt characterized imperial Rome. This does not do justice to the various facts. While it is true that Romans from Rome remained persistently snobbish about the presence of outsiders in political life, the emperors, especially the Flavians, supported the entry into the Senate of provincials—initially from nearby provinces such as Gaul and Spain, but eventually from the Near East—and appointed them to senior military, government, and imperial posts. Indeed, from the second century AD onward a high proportion of emperors themselves were from the provinces. All that I know about this subject I owe to my Oxford colleague, Dr. Teresa Morgan.

38. Ibid., 102.

Julius Caesar guaranteed them certain privileges, which Augustus confirmed.[39] The Roman empire was not all of one, racist, anti-semitic piece.

V. The Moral Ambiguity of Empire

Insofar as "imperialism" is racist, oppressive, and exploitative *by definition*, the Bible—especially in the prophetic reaches of the Old Testament and in the New Testament—is "anti-imperialist." Unlike Gottwald, Horsley, and Elliott, however, the Bible does not assume that what is actual is always typical, that empire is always and everywhere "imperialist." Nor does it assume that centralized and hierarchical government, which can assume imperial dimensions, is intrinsically evil. That has been the main thrust of my argument so far. In the little space that remains, I want to begin reflect further on the moral ambiguity of empire, on its possible benefits as well as its possible evils, and then to conclude by considering when nations should and should not secede from it. What I shall have in mind, mainly, is the British empire.

First of all, let it be said plainly that empire *can* cause evils—for example, the displacement of native peoples in North America and Australia. To be the cause of an evil, however, is not yet to be responsible or culpable for it. Culpability requires malicious or careless intention. When the first Britons pitched camp down-under in Botany Bay, they did not intend to displace the aboriginal peoples. Indeed it took them some time to appreciate that the natives had a concept of property at all, and that what seemed to them virgin territory—unoccupied, uncultivated, and unproductive—was viewed by the natives as belonging to them (in a certain sense). That then raises the question—not, I think, readily tractable—of the extent to which one people is morally obliged not to settle and cultivate and render fruitful land, whose significance for another people is not so much economic as mythological.

Sometimes, however, evils are caused culpably. But that raises the question of who, exactly, is to blame. When British settlers abducted aboriginal women and children in Tasmania early in the nineteenth century, their actions were roundly condemned by their government. In 1814 Governor Thomas Davey issued a proclamation expressing "utter indignation and abhorrence" at the kidnapping of the children, and in 1819 Governor

---

39. Ibid., 102.

William Sorell ordered that abducted children should be supported at government expense.

However culpable the imperial government was for the fate of aboriginal Tasmanians, in the case of aboriginal Americans it had sought to protect them from the depredations of European colonists by raising money to station troops along the Appalachian frontier, as much to keep the colonists in as to keep the natives out. However, as I have already mentioned, the colonists were having none of it. I do not doubt that British motives in promising to preserve Indian lands from further invasion were mixed and considerably financial: London seriously did not want to incur the costs of yet more war. Nevertheless, this is one instance of a recurrent dynamic in the history of the British empire: one where the imperial centre exercises—or tries to exercise—a constraining influence on settlers, sometimes for reasons of humanity and justice toward natives. Thus it is often said that native-Americans got a better deal under Queen Victoria than they did under the Government of the Republic of Liberty to the south, because Canadian frontiersmen were restrained by imperial Westminster, whose views were not so closely identified with those of the settlers. Similarly, General Dyer's fateful decision in 1919 to open fire, without immediate warning, on an unarmed crowd in Amritsar attracted far more censure in liberal, imperial London than it did in paranoid Anglo-India.[40] Sometimes, then, the physical and cultural distance of an empire's centre from its periphery can constitute a positive moral advantage, removing it from the dominant influence of myopic local interests and prejudices and enabling a certain impartiality. And in case one doubts that imperial government's constraint of settlers could ever *really* have been motivated by care for humanity and justice toward natives—as distinct from, say, the financial costs of frontier strife—then one should recall that for much of the nineteenth century the Royal Navy devoted considerable resources to the suppression of the slave trade, of which it was the main, sometimes the only, opponent.

One obvious apparent problem with empire is that it comprises the imposition of rule by one people upon another, and so involves oppression and exploitation. The imposition of rule, however, is not inherently unjust: all government involves the threat and exercise of coercion against the unwilling, and good government involves just coercion against the unjustly unwilling. Nor is the oppression and exploitation of one group by another peculiar to empires: it happens within nation-states, too, whether

---

40. See Collett, *The Butcher of Amritsar*.

of social inferiors by their superiors, of minorities by majorities, or of one race by another. And, if the Acts of the Apostles is anything to go by, it even happens within churches.[41] Sometimes the imposition of imperial rule can have the salutary effect of imposing a unifying, pacific, and law-abiding order on peoples otherwise inclined to war among themselves. The order that an empire brings should not be instantly dismissed as intolerably unjust. It might be. On the other hand, sometimes a measure of injustice should be tolerated for the sake of a decent measure of peace, without which nothing at all can flourish. That can only be doubted by those who have been privileged to take peace entirely for granted.

But surely imperial rule is wrong because it interferes with the legitimate traditions and institutions of subject peoples? Not always. Much of British rule in India and Africa was remote and indirect, cooperating with traditional rulers and leaving them, within limits, free to do as they had always done. Presumably that should win the colonial authorities credit from those postmodernists who think that all cultures are morally equal—although it probably does not. More probably it did win them credit from those contemporaries who were happily unburdened by any sense of vocation to civilize the world, and from those who prudently recognized that the British simply lacked boots on the ground to do it. At the same time, of course, it also attracted the complaints of others, be they metropolitan liberals, Christian missionaries, or the nationalists they educated, who reckoned that some ways are in fact morally superior to others, and who judged the colonial authorities negligent, because they did not interfere *enough* to suppress authentically barbaric traditions, such as the self-immolation of widows. And when imperial authorities did interfere benevolently to better the lot of the rural poor, as did Lord Cromer in late nineteenth-century Egypt and the colonial administration in the Sudan between the two World Wars, they attracted the resentment of native elites, who touchily resented their subordination to foreign masters.[42]

This brings us to the first of two characteristic features of empire that make it prone to injustice: the domination of government by people who are culturally alien to those they govern. This need not go wrong, if the dominant group's commitment is long-term enough to allow them the patience

---

41. I am thinking here of Acts 6, which speaks of tension between Greek and Hebrew Christians in Jerusalem, because the latter gave preference to their own kind in the distribution of food from the common fund.

42. See Robert O. Collins and Francis Deng, *The British in the Sudan, 1898–1956*.

to respect those they seek to change; if they are willing to admit natives to government according to their merit; if they are therefore willing, in the end, to cede control; and if the natives are willing to trust them. Those are a lot of "ifs." The problems arise when the ruling people is determined to remain on top, come what may, and especially when their determination is motivated by a racist contempt for those they rule. Racist contempt is not always born of sheer malice; sometimes it is the natural child of frustration, impatience, and fear—as American troops fighting insurgency in Iraq and Afghanistan have discovered. But whatever its provenance, it is fatal. In this respect, British rule in India was ambivalent. On the one hand, there was the liberal impulse to induct Indians into the admirable ways of British public administration and law; but on the other hand, there was the fear of losing control, which, combined with doubts about native fitness, fueled an ugly and offensive contempt. So when in 1883 the Viceroy, Lord Ripon, proposed to extend the jurisdiction of Indian local magistrates to cover cases involving Europeans, he provoked a violent reaction from British residents, and was forced to withdraw his proposal.[43]

The second moral weakness of empire is a function of its geographical extent. At least in the case of far-flung, geographically scattered empires (like the British one) very different places generate significantly different needs, practices, traditions, and identities. This obviously creates a practical problem for imperial cohesion; but this practical problem can easily become the occasion for a moral-political one. This is because geographical distance tends to diminish sympathetic understanding; and so imperial centres, well intentioned but ill informed, are prone to make judgements, laws, and policies that *do not fit the circumstances* of colonies on the far side of the world. As I have already mentioned, this is what happened in the case of the British colonies in America in the eighteenth century, where a cultural gap opened up that was visible in the French and Indian War, and then became flammable in 1775.

VI. The Moral Ambiguity of Anti-imperialism

Empire is often a complex and morally ambiguous phenomenon. So is nationalist anti-imperialism. I do not doubt that imperial rule—like any other kind of rule—can be oppressive and deserve opposition. Nor do I doubt that it can become so consistently, gravely, and resolutely oppressive

43. James, *The Rise and Fall of the British Empire*, 231.

Nationalism and Empire

as to warrant repudiation, sometimes by way of armed resistance. Nevertheless, nationalist, anti-imperialist separatism is not its own justification. Sometimes it is moved by past grievances rather than present ones, and mistakes the fetish of national independence for the substantive welfare of the people. Sometimes it is fueled by private ambition rather than public concern. Often it is manned by young men, hungry for adventure and spoiling for a fight—as young men typically are.

Take, for example, Ireland between 1916 and 1921. This was the first case of secession from the British empire since 1783. It was a major source of inspiration for Indian nationalism: Nehru visited Dublin in 1916. And the guerrilla tactics employed by the Irish Republican Army (I.R.A.) became a model for nationalist resistance movements worldwide. The so-called Irish War of Independence[44] began with the Easter Rising of 1916. Was the uprising justified?

According to the Christian tradition of "just war" reasoning, the justification of the use of armed force depends on at least the following four criteria: that it is a response to a grave injustice ("just cause"); that it intends to fend off and correct that injustice ("right intention"); that it is a "last resort," undertaken only when all peaceful and feasible means of remedy have been exhausted; and that it is undertaken by a "legitimate authority."[45] What grave and persistent injustice beyond any peaceful remedy did the Easter Rising aim to fend off and correct? None at all. Ireland had had direct representation in the Westminster parliament since 1801, and the minority of Irish M.P.s there was sufficiently large and vociferous to keep Irish issues at the forefront of parliamentary business in the latter decades of the nineteenth century and the opening ones of the twentieth. Consequently, by 1916 all of the major substantive grievances against British-dominated government had been addressed. In 1829 the Catholic Emancipation Act

---

44. I say "so-called" because the title, "Irish War of Independence," connotes a degree of unanimity among the Irish people that did not exist. The conflict of 1916–21 did not simply pitch the Irish against the British. It set Irishman against Irishman. One man's "war of independence" is usually another man's "civil war."

45. I refer here specifically to *Christian* "just war" reasoning, because it differs in at least one basic respect from certain modern philosophical versions. According to the Christian tradition, the just use of force is basically a punitive reaction to grave injustice. Whether it is a defensive or aggressive reaction is beside the moral point. In versions of "just war" reasoning that take their cue from the U.N. Charter, however, just cause for war is self-defence against aggression. This is what David Rodin, for example, takes to be "just war" reasoning in *War and Self-Defense*. For further discussion of this, see Biggar, *In Defence of War*, chapter 5.

had ended the legal exclusion of Catholics from public office. By the close of the century Protestant control of government in Ireland had been largely removed: the majority of Irish judges and senior officers in the Dublin Metropolitan Police and the Royal Irish Constabulary were of Catholic, nationalist stock.[46] In 1903 the Wyndham Act had addressed the chronic vulnerability of tenant farmers by providing them with government funds to purchase land from their landlords, resulting in a majority of them becoming landowners. Further, Ireland was enjoying a cultural renaissance; and, while her per capita national product was less than two-thirds that of the rest of the United Kingdom, it was higher than that of Norway, Sweden, Italy, and Finland, and only 7.6 percent behind that of France.[47] Further still, a measure of "home rule" had been on the Westminster statute book since 1914, awaiting implementation at the war's end. For sure, such implementation was rendered uncertain by the threat of armed resistance from Protestants in northern Ireland, but the outcome had not been determined and success was still possible. Therefore, there was no persistent, grave injustice to justify the 1916 rebels' attempt to seize independence by force of arms. What there was instead was a belief in the cathartic property of nationalist bloodshed, an atavistic hatred of the British connection, and a revolutionary élite's fear that the Irish people were becoming decadent in their contentment with it.[48]

Tragically, the Rising did indeed succeed in provoking intermittent bouts of military repression by the Government, whose severity served to alienate Irish hearts and minds. In 1919 the Irish Republican Army launched a guerrilla war with the killing of two armed policemen. The British military response culminated in the infamous campaign of the "Black-and-Tans," whose indiscriminate reprisals against a population that many of them had come to loathe had the counterproductive result that the loyalty of most Irish people shifted to the nascent institutions of republican

---

46. For a local level account of the dismantling of the Protestant Ascendancy before 1910, see Dooley, *The Plight of Monaghan Protestants, 1912–1926*, 7–19. I should make it clear that, when I write here of judges and police being "nationalist," I do not mean to say that they supported secession. Most Irish nationalists before 1916 supported "home rule" within the British empire.

47. See Lee, *Ireland, 1912–1985*, 513, Table 12.

48. Patrick Pearse's faith in the redemptive power of the blood of nationalist martyrs is famous: see, e.g., Dudley Edwards, *Patrick Pearse*, 179. For evidence that anxiety about terminal Irish decadence was among the motives that impelled the 1916 rebels, see, e.g., FitzGerald, *Desmond's Rising*, 58–59, 88.

Nationalism and Empire

rule.⁴⁹ It is true, of course, that the rampaging of the "Black-and Tans" was partly a reaction to the I.R.A.'s aggressive⁵⁰ campaign of assassination and guerrilla warfare, which was itself less than scrupulously discriminate,⁵¹ erasing the distinction between combatants and civilians. It is also true that their rampaging was not the government's policy.⁵² It was, however, its responsibility. By failing to prevent it, the government lost the power to win back popular trust, and could only have clawed back popular compliance by the use of force on a massive scale that, being unpopular in England and therefore politically unsustainable, would have been disproportionate. The government had lost legitimate political authority both as a moral claim and as a social fact.⁵³ By the time of the Anglo-Irish Treaty of December 1921, the republican movement, for all its moral ambiguities, had acquired the political power to govern better.

Notwithstanding this, judging in terms of the criteria of just cause, right intention, and last resort, Ireland's Easter Rising of 1916—a famous and seminal instance of nationalist revolt against imperial government and in favour of national independence—was not justified. If empires are bound to give a morally justifying account of themselves, then so are anti-imperialist movements. Sometimes the former can succeed; sometimes the latter can fail.

V. Conclusion

I hope it is clear that my intention in this closing chapter has not been to defend "imperialism." How could I defend it, since by definition and connotation it is immoral? "Imperialism" is no more morally defensible than "torture." What I *have* sought to do, however, is to make a persuasive

---

49. The title "Black-and-Tans" refers to two bodies of policemen commonly characterized by their motley uniforms. The first comprised English and Scottish veterans of the Great War, who were recruited into the Royal Irish Constabulary (R.I.C.) from January 1920; the second, members of the R.I.C.'s Auxiliary Division. The latter were responsible for most of the outrages. (I thank William Sheehan for helping me get these details right.) See Peter Hart's contemporary classic, *The I.R.A. and Its Enemies*, 4, 81–83, 118.

50. According to Richard English, in his widely praised *Irish Freedom*, 287: "There is no doubt that republicans were the aggressors in this war [of 1919–21]."

51. See Hart, *The I.R.A. and Its Enemies*, especially Part IV, "Neighbours and Enemies."

52. See Sheehan, *A Hard Local War*.

53. I have developed this distinction in "Christian Just War Reasoning and Two Cases of Rebellion: Ireland 1916–1921 and Syria 2011–Present."

argument that the historical reality of empire has not always lived down to its imperialist stereotype, and that it has even displayed some noteworthy virtues. I have also sought to muddy the genealogical and moral waters between empire and nation-state. I have done this, in order to make the case that nationalist revolts against empire, which aim to establish independent nation-states, are not intrinsically justified, since empire need not constitute intolerable injustice. Nationalism, even when anti-imperialist, is bound to render a cogent moral account of itself.

Conclusion

National loyalty, nations, and nation-states are here to stay for the foreseeable future. That is a political fact. Human loyalties have long reached well beyond kin, while cosmopolis still refuses to descend to earth from the realm of (supposed) ideals.

But nations and nation-states are not just political facts; they are morally significant facts. They deserve loyalty insofar as their customs and institutions embody an understanding of what makes for human flourishing—and all nations embody *some* such understanding. Further, because different nations in different places with different histories are bound to develop distinctive insights into the social forms that defend and promote human flourishing, they deserve a measure of autonomy. And they deserve this for the sake of the common good; for what one nation discovers, others might profit from. This national autonomy, therefore, is not a morality-free space. It is not simply or primarily a space for consumers to satisfy whatever happens to be their preference. Rather, it is a space for the development of a particular version of the good life. If this sounds chillingly, illiberally monistic, it need not. Probably, and in a large national society certainly, a particular version of the good life will contain rival sub-versions. Unity can contain lively plurality.

So understood, national autonomy deserves to be defended, if not at all costs. One threat that needs to be fended off is the immigration of peoples, whose own version of the good life is significantly alien, on such a scale as to threaten significant law-breaking or even the political viability of the host nation's customs and institutions. Borders ought to be policed, therefore, and immigration controlled.

Another threat is related, but internal rather than external: the rising to cultural dominance of a worldview that generates a version of the good life that is degrading of human dignity and subversive of basic human equality. This warrants the nation-state's affirmation of a public orthodoxy that is humanist. In a society whose members adhere to a diversity of religions and philosophies, such an orthodoxy will have to be liberal, in the sense of "generously capacious," if it is to win sufficient popular support to be politically sustainable. Exactly what kind of liberal, humanist orthodoxy should prevail, will vary according to the history and traditions of different nations.

National autonomy is valuable only as a means, not in itself. It is valuable only as a condition of the development of a particular, and more or less distinctive, version of the good life. Therefore, it cannot be used to claim immunity from interference in case of a state's persistent, systemic perpetration of atrocious and massive oppression of its own people. National autonomy, as I have defended it, is not the same as legal sovereignty. As a nation-state has a responsibility to care for the flourishing of all its people, and therefore to treat them justly, so it has a responsibility (if it has the power) to intervene against another state's gross abuse. At best, such humanitarian interference should be authorized by the U.N. Security Council. However, should the Council's political paralysis preclude this, intervention might still be morally justified.

It is right that nations should enjoy a measure of autonomy. It is not always right that they should seek to increase it. *Pace* the siren gospel of Romantic nationalism, it is not written in heaven that every nation should achieve maximal independence or sovereignty. Contemporary Scottish nationalists, for example, are misled and misleading to talk of secession from the United Kingdom as the natural completion of Scotland's "journey." The clearest justification of national independence is where the nation suffers grave injustice that cannot be remedied under a lesser level of autonomy. A sufficient justification is where the nation could flourish significantly better, were it independent, and where its becoming so would not wrong its former compatriots. But whatever the moral justification, separatist nationalists are obliged to furnish a cogent one—even when they are anti-imperialist. National independence can be a fetish, and a fetish is a false god.

Bibliography

Ahdar, Rex, and Ian Leigh. *Religious Freedom in the Liberal State*. Oxford: Oxford University Press, 2005.
Anderson, Benedict. *Imagined Communities: Reflections on the Origin and Spread of Nationalism*. Rev. ed. New York: Verso, 1991.
Anderson, Fred. *Crucible of War: The Seven Years' War and the Fate of the Empire in British North America, 1754–1766*. London: Faber, 2001.
Anstey, Roger. *The Atlantic Slave Trade and British Abolition, 1760–1810*. Cambridge Commonwealth Series. London: MacMillan, 1975.
Aquinas, Thomas. *Summa Theologiae*. Blackfriars edition. London: Eyre and Spottiswoode, 1964.
Arnold, Matthew. *Mixed Essays*. London: Smith, Elder & Co., 1880.
Ashworth, Jacinta, and Ian Farthing. *Churchgoing in the UK*. London: Tearfund, 2007.
Barth, Karl. *Church Dogmatics*. 4 vols. Vol. III, *The Doctrine of Creation*, Part 4, "The Command of God the Creator." Edited by G. W. Bromiley and T. F. Torrance. Edinburgh: T. & T. Clark, 1961.
Bayne, T. W. "Tulloch, John." In *Oxford Dictionary of National Biography*. Revised by H. C. G. Matthew. Oxford: Oxford University Press, 2004–10.
Bellamy, Alex J. *Responsibility to Protect: The Global Effort to End Mass Atrocities*. Cambridge: Polity, 2009.
Bennett, J. Harry. *Bondsmen and Bishops: Slavery and Apprenticeship on the Codrington Plantation in Barbados, 1710–1838*. University of California Publications in History, Vol. LXII. Berkeley: University of California, 1958.
Biggar, Nigel. "Christian Just War Reasoning and Two Cases of Rebellion: Ireland 1916–1921 and Syria 2011–Present." *Ethics and International Affairs* 27.4 (2013) 393–400.
———. *In Defence of War*. Oxford: Oxford University Press, 2013.
———. "Melting the Icepacks of Enmity: Forgiveness and Reconciliation in Northern Ireland." *Studies in Christian Ethics* 24.2 (2011) 199–209.
———. "Not Translation, but Conversation: Theology in Public Debate about Euthanasia." In *Religious Voices in Public Places*, edited by Nigel Biggar and Linda Hogan, 151–93. Oxford: Oxford University Press, 2009.
———. "A Reply to Theo Hobson." *Theology* 115.3 (May/June 2012) 175–79.
Biggar, Nigel, and Linda Hogan, editors. *Religious Voices in Public Places*. Oxford: Oxford University Press, 2009.

Bibliography

Blair, Tony. "Full Statement to the House of Commons, 18 March 2003." In *A Matter of Principle: Humanitarian Arguments for War in Iraq*, edited by Thomas Cushman, 329–39. Berkeley, CA: University of California, 2005.
Bolt, Robert. *A Man for All Seasons*. London: Heinemann, 1960.
Brandon, S. G. F. *Jesus and the Zealots: A Study of the Political Factor in Primitive Christianity*. Manchester: Manchester University Press, 1967.
Carey, Lucius. *Sir Lucius Cary, late Lord Viscount of Falkland, his discourse of infallibility, with an answer to it: and his Lordships reply. Never before published. Together with Mr. Walter Mountague's letter concerning the changing his religion*. Edited by Thomas Triplet. London: Gartrude Dawson, 1651.
Carter, Warren. *Matthew and Empire: Initial Explorations*. Harrisburg, PA: Trinity, 2001.
Clements, Keith. *True Patriotism: Love of Country in Dialogue with the Witness of Dietrich Bonhoeffer*. London: Collins, 1986.
Coffey, John. "The Abolition of the Slave Trade: Christian Conscience and Political Action." *Cambridge Papers* 15.1. Cambridge: Jubilee Centre, 2006.
Collett, Nigel. *The Butcher of Amritsar: General Reginald Dyer*. London: Hambledon, 2005.
Colley, Linda. *Britons: Forging the Nation, 1707–1837*. New Haven: Yale University Press, 2005.
Collier, Paul. *Exodus: Immigration and Multiculturalism in the 21st Century*. London: Allen Lane, 2013.
Collins, Adela Yarbro. *Mark: A Commentary*. Hermaneia. Minneapolis: Fortress, 2007.
Collins, Robert O., and Francis Deng. *The British in the Sudan, 1898–1956*. London: MacMillan, 1984.
Cowell, Alan. "Al Jazeera Video Links London Bombings to Al Qaeda." *New York Times*, 2 September 2005.
Cranmer, Frank, John Lucas, and Bob Morris. *Church and State: A Mapping Exercise*. London: The Constitution Unit, University College London, 2006.
Crawshaw, Steve. "A Journey into the Unknown." *The Independent on Sunday*, 28 March 1999.
Creighton, Mandell. "Chillingworth, William." In *Dictionary of National Biography*, vol. X, edited by Leslie Stephen, 256–57. London: Smith, Elder, & Co., 1886.
Crossan, John Dominic, and Jonathan L. Reed. *In Search of Paul: How Jesus' Apostle Opposed Rome's Empire with God's Kingdom*. New York: HarperSanFrancisco, 2005.
Curtice, John, and Rachel Ormston. "On the Road to Divergence? Trends in Public Opinion in Scotland and England." In *British Social Attitudes 28*, edited by Alison Parks et al., 21–36. National Centre for Social Research. London: Sage, 2012.
Davis, David Brion. "An Appreciation of Roger Anstey." In *Anti-Slavery, Religion, and Reform: Essays in Memory of Roger Anstey*, edited by Christine Bolt and Seymour Drescher, 11–17. Folkestone, UK: Dawson, 1980.
Dooley, Terence. *The Plight of Monaghan Protestants, 1912–1926*. Maynooth Studies in Irish Local History. Dublin: Irish Academic Press, 2000.
Dudley Edwards, Ruth. *Patrick Pearse: The Triumph of Failure*. Dublin: Swords, 1990.
Elite UK Forces. "Special Air Service (SAS)—Operation Barras—Sierra Leone." Online: http://www.eliteukforces.info/special-air-service/sas-operations/operation-barras/.
Elliott, Neil. "The Apostle Paul and Empire." In *In the Shadow of Empire*, edited by Richard Horsley, 97–116. Louisville: Westminster John Knox, 2008.
———. *The Arrogance of Nations: Reading Romans in the Shadow of Empire*. Minneapolis: Fortress, 2008.

Bibliography

English, Richard. *Irish Freedom: The History of Nationalism in Ireland.* London: Macmillan, 2006.

Evans, Gareth. *The Responsibility to Protect. Ending Mass Atrocity Crimes Once and for All.* Washington, DC: Brookings Institute, 2008.

Fichte, J. G. *Addresses to the German Nation.* Chicago: Open Court, 1922.

FitzGerald, Desmond. *Desmond's Rising: Memoirs 1913 to Easter 1916.* Rev. ed. Dublin: Liberties, 2006

Gaita, Raymond. *A Common Humanity.* London: Routledge, 2000.

Garton Ash, Timothy. "What Young British Muslims Say Can Be Shocking—Some of It Is Also True." *The Guardian*, 10 August 2006.

Goodhart, David. *The British Dream: Successes and Failures of Post-War Immigration.* London: Atlantic, 2013.

Gottwald, Norman K. "Early Israel as an Anti-Imperial Community." In *In the Shadow of Empire*, edited by Richard Horsley, 9–24. Louisville: Westminster John Knox, 2008.

Griffin, Martin. *Latitudinarianism in the Seventeenth-Century Church of England.* Annotated by Richard Popkin; edited by Lila Freedman. Studies in Intellectual History, vol. 32. Leiden: Brill, 1992.

Grotius, Hugo. *The Rights of War and Peace.* 3 vols. Edited by Richard Tuck. Indianapolis: Liberty Fund, 2005.

Guelich, Robert. *Mark 1:1—8:26.* Word Biblical Commentary 34a. Dallas: Word, 1989.

Habermas, Jürgen. "Habermas entre démocratie et génétique." *Le Monde*, 20 December 2002.

Harpsfield, Nicholas. *The Life and Death of Sir Thomas Moore, Knight, Sometymes Lord High Chancellor of England.* Edited by E. V. Hitchcock and R. W. Chambers. Early English Text Society, Original Series, no. 186. London: Oxford University Press, 1932.

Hart, Peter. *The I.R.A. and Its Enemies: Violence and Community in Cork, 1916–1923.* Oxford: Clarendon, 1998.

Hastings, Adrian. *The Construction of Nationhood: Ethnicity, Religion, and Nationalism.* Cambridge: Cambridge University Press, 1997.

Henson, Hensley. *Christian Morality: Natural, Developing, Final.* Gifford Lectures 1935–36. Oxford: Clarendon, 1936.

Hobson, Theo. "Establishment and Liberalism: A Response to Nigel Biggar." *Theology* 115.3 (2012) 163–74.

Hooker, Morna D. *The Gospel according to St Mark.* Black's New Testament Commentaries. London: Black, 1991.

Hooker, Richard. *Of the Laws of Ecclesiastical Polity.* In *The Works of Mr Richard Hooker*, edited by John Keble. 3 vols. Oxford: Clarendon, 1874.

Horsley, Richard A., editor. *In the Shadow of Empire: Reclaiming the Bible as a History of Faithful Resistance.* Louisville: Westminster John Knox, 2008.

———. *Jesus and Empire: The Kingdom of God and the New World Disorder.* Minneapolis: Fortress, 2003.

———, editor. *Paul and Empire: Religion and Power in Roman Imperial History.* Harrisburg, PA: Trinity, 1997.

Husain, Ed. *The Islamist.* London: Penguin, 2007.

Hyde, Edward (Earl of Clarendon). *Animadversions upon a book, intituled, Fanaticism fanatically imputed to the Catholic Church, by Dr Stillingfleet, and the imputation*

Bibliography

refuted and retorted by S. C., by a person of honour. 2nd ed. London: R. Royston, 1674.
International Commission on Intervention and State Sovereignty (ICISS). *The Responsibility to Protect*. Ottawa: International Development Research Centre, 2001.
Jakobsson, Stiv. *Am I Not a Man and a Brother? British Missions and the Abolition of the Slave trade and Slavery in West Africa and the West Indies, 1786–1838*. Studia Missionalia Upsaliensia XVII. Lund: Gleerup, 1972.
James, Lawrence. *The Rise and Fall of the British Empire*. London: Abacus, 1994.
Ketcham, Ralph. *James Madison: A Biography*. Charlottesville, VA: University of Virginia, 1990.
Kidd, Colin. *Union and Unionisms: Political Thought in Scotland, 1500–2000*. Cambridge: Cambridge University Press, 2008.
Lane, William L. *The Gospel of Mark*. The New London Commentary on the New Testament. London: Marshall, Morgan and Scott, 1974.
Lee, J. J. *Ireland, 1912–1985: Politics and Society*. Cambridge: Cambridge University Press, 1989.
Malik, Shiv. "My Brother the Bomber." *Prospect*, June 2007.
Maurice, F. D. *Social Morality*. London: Macmillan, 1893.
Methodist Church (in Britain). *Report on Church, State, and Establishment*. Peterborough, UK: Methodist, 2004.
Miller, David. *On Nationality*. Oxford: Clarendon, 1995.
Miller, David, and Sohail Hashmi, editors. *Boundaries and Justice: Diverse Ethical Perspectives*. Ethikon Series in Comparative Ethics. Princeton: Princeton University Press, 2001.
Miller, Richard. "Christian Attitudes towards Boundaries: Metaphysical and Geographical." In *Boundaries and Justice*, edited by David Miller and Sohail Hashmi, 15–37. Princeton: Princeton University Press, 2001.
Modood, Tariq. *Church, State, and Religious Minorities*. London: Policy Studies Institute, 1997.
———. "Establishment, Multiculturalism, and British Citizenship." *Political Quarterly* 65.1 (1994) 53–73.
Moltke, Helmuth James von. *Letters to Freya: A Witness against Hitler*. London: Collins Harvill, 1991.
Morris, R. M., editor. *Church and State in 21st Century Britain: The Future of Church Establishment*. Basingstoke, UK: Palgrave Macmillan, 2009.
Nicholls, O. P., Aidan. *The Realm: An Unfashionable Essay on the Conversion of England*. Oxford: Family, 2008.
Norman, Edward. *Secularisation*. London: Continuum, 2003.
Nussbaum, Martha. *Liberty of Conscience: In Defense of America's Tradition of Religious Equality*. New York: Basic, 2008.
Nygren, Anders. *Agape and Eros*. Translated by Philip S. Watson. Chicago: University of Chicago Press, 1982.
O'Donovan, Oliver. *The Desire of the Nations: Rediscovering the Roots of Political Theology*. Cambridge: Cambridge University Press, 1986.
Owen, Roger. *Lord Cromer: Victorian Imperialist, Edwardian Proconsul*. Oxford: Oxford University Press, 2004.
Park, Alison, et al., editors. *British Social Attitudes: The 26th Report*. London: Sage, 2010.

Bibliography

Perry, Michael J. *Under God? Religious Faith and Liberal Democracy.* Cambridge: Cambridge University Press, 2003.
Pfizenmaier, Thomas C. *The Trinitarian Theology of Dr Samuel Clarke (1675–1729). Context, Sources, Controversy.* Studies in the History of Christian Thought, vol. LXXV. Leiden: Brill, 1997.
Pigott, Robert. "Faith Diary." BBC News website. 24 Feb 2009. Online: http://news.bbc.co.uk/1/hi/uk/7783563.stm.
———. "Public 'Favour Religious Values.'" 25 Feb 2009. Online: http://news.bbc.co.uk/1/hi/uk/7906595.stm.
Rawls, John. *Political Liberalism.* New York: Columbia University Press, 1996.
Rees-Mogg, William. "Reform the Monarchy? Let's Wait for a Century." *The Times,* 30 March 2009.
Reynolds, David. *America, Empire of Liberty: A New History.* London: Penguin, 2010.
Rodin, David. *War and Self-Defense.* Oxford: Clarendon, 2002.
Russell, Meg. *Reforming the House of Lords: Lessons from Overseas.* Oxford: Oxford University Press, 2000.
Sheehan, William. *A Hard Local War: The British Army and the Guerrilla War in Ireland, 1919–1922.* Stroud, UK: The History Press, 2011.
Stiltner, Brian, and Steven Michels. "Religion, Rhetoric, and Running for Office: Public Reason on the US Campaign Trail." In *Religious Voices in Public Places,* edited by Nigel Biggar and Linda Hogan, 260–85. Oxford: Oxford University Press, 2009.
Suárez, Francisco. *A Work on the Three Theological Virtues, Faith, Hope, and Charity* [1621]: "On Charity: Disputation XIII." In *Selections from Three Works,* by Francisco Suárez, S.J., 2 vols. Vol. II: "The Translation," edited by Gwladys L. Williams et al. The Classics of International Law. Oxford: Clarendon, 1944.
Taylor, Charles. "The Politics of Recognition." In *Multiculturalism: Examining the Politics of Recognition,* edited by Amy Gutman, 25–73. Princeton: Princeton University Press, 1994.
Temple, William. *Christianity and the State.* Henry Scott Holland Memorial Lectures 1928. London: Macmillan, 1928.
Torrance, David. *Salmond against the Odds.* Edinburgh: Birlinn, 2011.
Trevor-Roper, Hugh. *Catholics, Anglicans, and Puritans: Seventeenth-Century Essays.* London: Fontana, 1989.
Tulloch, John. *Rational Theology and Christian Philosophy in England in the 17th Century.* 2 vols. Vol. I, "Liberal Churchmen." 2nd ed. 1874. Reprint. Hildesheim, Germany: Olms, 1966.
Vitoria, Francisco de. "On Dietary Laws, or Self-Restraint." In *Political Writings,* edited by Anthony Pagden and Jeremy Lawrance, 205–30. Cambridge Texts in the History of Political Thought. Cambridge: Cambridge University Press, 1991.
Walker, Graham. "Illusory Pluralism, Inexorable Establishment." In *Obligations of Citizenship and Demands of Faith: Religious Accommodation in Pluralist Democracies.* edited by Nancy L. Rosenblum, 111–26. Princeton: Princeton University Press, 2000.
Watt, Nicholas. "Scottish Independence Referendum: Salmond Attacks UK's 'Bullying Tactics.'" *The Guardian,* 13 January 2012. Online: www.theguardian.com/politics/2012/jan/13/salmond-attacks-bullying-tactics-scotland.
Weller, Paul. *Time for a Change: Reconfiguring Religion, State, and Society.* New York: Continuum, 2005.

Bibliography

Westermann, Claus. *Genesis 1-11: a Commentary.* Translated by John J. Scullion, S.J. London: SPCK, 1984.

Wolterstorff, Nicholas. "Why Can't We All Just Get Along with Each Other?" In *Religious Voices in Public Places*, edited by Nigel Biggar and Linda Hogan, 17-36. Oxford: Oxford University Press, 2009.

Yevtushenko, Yevgeni. "Babii Yar." In *The Collected Poems, 1952-90*, 102-4. Edinburgh: Mainstream, 1991.

General Index

agape, 3–4
Ahdar, Rex, 45
A Man for All Seasons, 58–59
American War of Independence
 (1775–83), 81–84, 92
Amritsar (1919), Massacre of, 40
Anderson, Benedict 7
Anglican establishment, 30–32,
 35–51, 52
 popular support for, 48–51
 and religious freedom, 44–45
 and slavery 38–39
 as liberal, 39–42
Anglo-Irish Treaty (1921), 95
Anstey, Roger, 39
anti-imperialism, 21–22, chapter 4
 passim
 moral ambiguity of, 92–95
Arnold, Matthew, 42
Ash, Timothy Garton, 27–28
Augustine, 28–29
Australia, 89–90

BBC poll (February 2009), 50
Babii Yar, 17n.44
Baring, Evelyn: *see* 'Cromer, Lord'
Barth, Karl, 8, 16–17
beneficence, 6
'Black and Tans', 94–95
Blair, Tony, 32, 59–60, 64
Bonhoeffer, Dietrich, 15
borders: *see* 'national borders'
Brandon, S. G. F., 79

Britain: *see* United Kingdom
British empire, 20n.48, 74, 80–84,
 89–95
 and suppression of slavery, 84, 90
British Social Attitudes (2008), 49–50
British Social Attitudes (2010), 23
Britishness, xiv
Brown, Gordon, xiv
Bulgaria, 11

Canada, 19, 90
Carey, Lucius, 40–42
Carter, Warren, 75
Chillingworth, William, 41–42
Christian ethics, xv–xvi
cohesion, national: *see* 'national
 cohesion'
Colley, Linda, xiv, 7
Collier, Paul, 18n.45
Collins, Adela Yarbro, 85
common good, responsibility for,
 14–15
coronation service, 31
cosmopolitanism, 1–2, 17, 69–70
 and Christianity 1–5, 15
 and Jesus 2, 3
 and Paul 2, 3–4, 15
creatureliness, 5–7, 17, 19
Cromer, Lord, 79, 83–84, 91
Crossan, John Dominic, 75
diversity, good of international
 10–13, 16, 53
 and Anglican tradition 12–13

General Index

and Pentecost, 11–12
and Tower of Babel 13
diversity, good of national, 26
diversity, religious, 26–27

Easter Rising (1916), 20n.48, 93, 95
Elliott, Neil, 75, 86–89
empire, 12, 13, 70, chapter 4 *passim*
    and biblical studies, 75–89
    and cultural interference, 91
    and moral ambiguity, 89–92
    and racism, 88, 92
empire, British: *see* 'British empire'
establishment of religion, 30–52
    Christian objection to, 32
    secularist objection to, 32–35
    and equal dignity, 45–46
    and religious freedom, 44–45
European Union, xiii, 70
Evans, Gareth, 69, 71nn.36 and 37

Faith in the City (1985), 32
Fichte, Johann Gottlieb, 7–8
forgiveness, 4–5

Gaita, Raymond, 43
Gallagher, Jim, 24n.55
global state, 69–70, 72
globalisation, xiii
Good Friday Agreement: *see*
    'Northern Ireland, and the
    Good Friday Agreement'
Goodhart, David, 1n.1, 18n.45
Gordon, Charles George, 84
Gottwald, Norman, 74–78
    and interpretative method, 77–78
Great Tew Circle, 40–42
Grotius, Hugo, 54–56, 57, 62, 72

Habermas, Jürgen, 43
Hastings, Adrian 10–11, 51n.71
Henson, Hensley, 13
hierarchy, 78
Hobbes, Thomas, 54, 56, 72
Hobson, Theo, 32n.8

Hooker, Morna D., 85n.30
Horsley, Richard, 75, 78–86
House of Lords, 31, 32
humanist ethos, chapter 2 *passim*
    and Christianity, 30, 36–37
Husain, Ed, 29–30

image of God, 5
immigration, 18, 25, 97
Incarnation of God, 4, 12
independence, national: *see* 'national
    independence'
India, British, 90, 92
international law: *see* 'national
    sovereignty, and international
    law'
Ireland, xv, 22, 24n.54, 36; 93–95; *see
    also* 'Northern Ireland'
Irish 'War of Independence', 20n.48,
    93–95

just war reasoning, Christian 93

Kantian moral idealism, 66
Khan, Mohammed Sidique, 27
Kidd, Colin, xvn.2
Kitchener, Herbert, 84
Kosovo, 19, 22, 64–65, 68, 71

Lane, William, 85n.30
legitimacy, political, 31
Leigh, Ian, 45
liberalism
    and need of humanism, 28–30,
        33–35
    and self-subversive
        libertarianism, 28–30, 33–34
    as public orthodoxy, 38, 52
loyalty, national: *see* 'national loyalty'

Madison, James, 82–83
Maurice, F. D., 12
Mazower, Mark, 11n.25
Meiwes, Armin, 34

106

General Index

Miller, D, xivn.1
Miller, Richard B, 2
Modood, Tariq, 44
Moltke, Helmuth James von, 15-16
Monarchy, 31-32, 44n.38
More, Sir Thomas, 16
Morris, R. M., 50, 51n.72
multiculturalism, 18n.45, 25, 52

nation, 7-9
    definition of, xiv-xv
    development of 8
    transience of, 7, 9, 18, 19, 25
    and incarnation of universal
        human goods, 9, 10, 15-16,
        25, 51-52, 53, 54, 97
    and responsibility for the
        common good, 14-17,19
    and 'the chosen people', 15
    and vocation 16
national borders 17-25, 97
national cohesion, 18, chapter 2
    passim, 97-98
national identity
    and Christianity 11-12, chapter
        2 *passim*
    and humanism, chapter 2 *passim*
    and Islam 11
national independence, xv, 21-22, 24,
    92-95, 98
national interest, the morality of,
    67-69
national loyalty, chapter 1 *passim*, 97
    as limited by moral obligation,
        14-15
national sovereignty, xv, 19, chapter
    3 *passim*
    and international law, 53-62,
        72-73
    and military intervention, 62-67
    and moral illegality, 62-71
    and natural law, 54-57
    see also 'national independence'
    and 'nation-state, and
        autonomy'

nationalism, 20-21
    definition of, xv
    Romantic, 7-8, 15, 98
    Scottish: *see* 'Scottish nationalism'
    and scapegoating myths, 20, 21,
        24
    and secularisation, 7-8
nation-state, 9
    definition of, xv
    and autonomy, xiv-xv, 9, 19,
        97-98
    see also 'national sovereignty'
natural law: *see* 'national sovereignty,
    and natural law'
Nehru, Jawaharlal, 93
Netherlands, 21-22
Nicholls, Aidan, 51n.71
Northern Ireland, 20-21
    and the Good Friday Agreement
        (1998), 20-21
Nussbaum, Martha, 37, 47-48, 52
Nygren, Anders, 3

O'Donovan, Oliver, 13
Opinion Business Research poll
    (2001), 49-50
Ottoman empire, disintegration of, 74

Pearse, Patrick, 94n.48
Perry, Michael, 36n.16, 45
Pinter, Harold, 64
public orthodoxy, inevitability of,
    37-38, 52, 98

Quebec Act (1774), 82, 83

Rawls, John, 32-35, 47, 52
reason, public, 34-35
Reed, Jonathan L., 75
Rees-Mogg, William, 51n.71
Responsibility to Protect ('R2P'): *see*
    'The Responsibility to Protect'
Ripon, Lord, 92
Russell, Meg, 31n.7

General Index

Salmond, Alex, 23–24, 24n.54
Scotland, xv, 9, 19, 22–25
Scottish independence referendum (2014), xiv, 22
Scottish National Party, xiv, 22–25
Scottish nationalism, xv, 22–25, 98
Sharp, Granville, 38
Sheldon, Gilbert, 41
Sierra Leone (2001), British intervention in, 68
sin, universality of, 20
Society for the Propagation of the Gospel (S.P.G.), 38–39
Suárez, Francisco, 57
Sudan, 91
suicide bombing in London on 7 July 2005, 27

Taylor, Charles, 46n.49
Tearfund, 48–49
Temple, William, 13
The Responsibility to Protect, 53–54n.1, 63–64, 70
Thomism, 54, 56, 66, 67–68
Trinity, God as, 12
Tulloch, John, 42

U.S.S.R., break-up of xiii, 20
United Kingdom, 7, 19
  'Cool Britannia' xiii
  and the European Union xiii, xiv
  as empire, 73
United States, 7, 19, 70, 76–77, 79, 80–84
  as empire, 73–74

Vitoria, Francisco de, 55, 57

Walker, Graham, 46n.48
Watkins, Peter, 24n.54
Weimar Republic, 31, 33
Weller, Paul, 46n.50, 51n.72
Wilberforce, William, 38
Williams, Rowan, 32
Wilson, Woodrow, 73
Witte, John, 45
Wolterstorff, Nicholas, 44

Yevtushenko, Yevgeni, 17
Yugoslavia, disintegration of, 74

Scripture Index

Genesis

1:4, 10, 12, 18, 21, 25, 31	56n.14
1:26–27	5–6.n16
11:1–9	12n.29

Matthew

8:5	2n.4
8:5–13	3n.13
8:22	2n.7
10:37	2n.6
12:46–50	2n.8
15:21–8	3n.13, 3n.14
22:30	56n.15
27:11–26	86
27:54	2n.4

Mark

3:31–35	2n.8
5:1–20	79
5:9	85
7:9–13	3n.12
12:13–17	79
12:31	56n.15
15:1–15	86
15:39	2n.4

Luke

7:3	2n.4
8:19–21	2n.8
9:60	2n.7
10:27	56n.15
14:26	2n.6
15:11–32	4–5
23:1–25	86
23:47	2n.4
23:47	2n.4

John

6:15	2n.3
18:28—19:16	86

Acts

2:4, 6	12n.28
6	91
25	87

Romans

13	87, 88

1 Corinthians

1:18, 25	88
2:6–8	87, 88
7	3n.9
12	88
15:24–25	87

Galatians

1:4	87
3:28	15

www.ingramcontent.com/pod-product-compliance
Lightning Source LLC
Chambersburg PA
CBHW030905170426
43193CB00009BA/736